WARRIOR • 135

# NORTH VIETNAMESE ARMY SOLDIER 1958–75

**GORDON L ROTTMAN**            ILLUSTRATED BY BRIAN DELF

First published in Great Britain in 2009 by Osprey Publishing,
Midland House, West Way, Botley, Oxford, OX2 0PH, UK
443 Park Avenue South, New York, NY 10016, USA
E-mail: info@ospreypublishing.com

A CIP catalog record for this book is available from the British Library.

ISBN-13: 978-184603-371-1
E-book ISBN: 978-184603-867-9

Editorial by Ilios Publishing, Oxford, UK (www.iliospublishing.com)
Page layout by Mark Holt
Index by Michael Forder
Typeset in Sabon and Myriad Pro
Originated by PDQ Media, Bungay, UK
Printed in China through Worldprint Ltd

09 10 11 12 13   10 9 8 7 6 5 4 3 2 1

FOR A CATALOG OF ALL BOOKS PUBLISHED BY OSPREY MILITARY AND
AVIATION PLEASE CONTACT:

NORTH AMERICA
Osprey Direct, c/o Random House Distribution Center, 400 Hahn Road,
Westminster, MD 21157
E-mail: info@ospreydirect.com

ALL OTHER REGIONS
Osprey Direct, The Book Service Ltd, Distribution Centre, Colchester Road,
Frating Green, Colchester, Essex, CO7 7DW,  UK
E-mail: info@ospreydirect.co.uk

**www.ospreypublishing.com**

## ACKNOWLEDGMENTS

The author is indebted to Ken Conboy, Steve Sherman and William Howard
for their assistance in providing information and materials.

## ARTIST'S NOTE

Readers may care to note that the original paintings from which the color
plates in this book were prepared are available for private sale.
The Publishers retain all reproduction copyright whatsoever. All enquiries
should be addressed to:

Brian Delf
7 Burcot Park
Burcot
Abingdon, OX14 3DH
UK

The Publishers regret that they can enter into no correspondence
upon this matter.

## THE WOODLAND TRUST

Osprey Publishing is supporting the Woodland Trust, the UK's leading
woodland conservation charity, by funding the dedication of trees.

## ABBREVIATIONS

| | |
|---|---|
| ARVN | Army of the Republic of Vietnam (pronounced "Are-van") |
| DKZ | *Dai-bac Khong Ziat* (recoilless rifle) |
| DRV | Democratic Republic of Vietnam (North Vietnam) |
| NLF | National Liberation Front |
| NVA | North Vietnamese Army |
| PAVN | People's Army of Vietnam |
| RVN | Republic of Vietnam (South Vietnam) |
| RPG | rocket-propelled grenade (RPG-2, RPG-7 – a.k.a. B40, B41) |
| US | United States |
| VC | Viet Cong |

**Front Cover Image:** "Fall of Saigon" © Jacques Pavlovsky/Sygma/Corbis

# CONTENTS

# NORTH VIETNAMESE ARMY SOLDIER 1958–75

## INTRODUCTION

What is commonly known as the North Vietnamese Army (NVA) or the People's Army of Vietnam (PAVN) – *Quan Doi Dang Dan* – was the regular army of the Democratic Republic of Vietnam (DRV) – *Viet Nam Dan Chu Cong Hoa* – or simply North Vietnam. In reality though there were actually two North Vietnamese armies. The homeland was defended by a conventional army equipped with armor and artillery and supported by an air force with jet aircraft, a small navy and paramilitary home defense forces. An even larger, what could be termed "expeditionary army," or rather an "army of liberation" conducting offensive operations, was sent to the South to support the National Front for the Liberation of South Vietnam (*Mat tran Dan toc Giai phong mien Nam Viet Nam*), or the National Liberation Front (NLF) and its armed insurgent force. This was the People's Liberation Armed Forces (PLAF) – *Quan Doi Giai Phong Nhan Dan* – or more commonly, the People's Liberation Army (PLA) – *Quan Doi Giai Phong* – otherwise known as the Viet Cong or VC.[1]

The North Vietnamese Army in South Vietnam – the Republic of Vietnam (RVN) – fought a conventional war, even though popular perception considered it a "guerrilla war." This impression was enhanced by the fact that it was supported by only limited artillery (substituted by mortars, rockets and recoilless rifles), armor and aviation support, that it operated without motorized vehicle support inside the RVN and that its troops were supported by VC guerrillas during their operations and used some guerrilla-like tactics and techniques themselves. However, the NVA actually fought a conventional war inside South Vietnam conducting regimental, divisional and corps-level operations. The NVA executed conventional tactics tailored to the terrain, climate and political situation and adapted to compensate for their limitations against the Free World Force's superior manpower, firepower and mobility. They did not generally hold terrain and lacked fixed bases and the logistical tail that so burdened Free World forces.

It was realized that a conventional war, along the lines of the 1950–53 Korean War, could not be fought in the south. That 37-month war cost China and North Korea over one million dead, missing, wounded and captured along with up to three million North Korean civilian dead. The DRV was

---

1 See Osprey Warrior 116, *Viet Cong Fighter* and Osprey Elite 38, *The NVA and Viet Cong.*

not willing, or able, to accept such casualties in a stand-up fight. Strategically, operationally and tactically there were valid reasons for not fighting a "traditional war" with frontlines and mobile logistics support. It was willing to take its time and fight a protracted war lasting many years. South Vietnam's much varied and rugged terrain and harsh climate, coupled with the Free World force's massive firepower, unprecedented mobility, lavish logistics system, widespread local security forces and highly mobile strike forces prevented the more lightly armed NVA from conducting a traditional war. Communist forces were handicapped by a long and fragile supply line from the north, limited mobility and the lengthy periods required to reconstitute battered units, and thus executed conventional tactics tailored to the terrain, climate, political situation and the capabilities of Free World forces.

The relationships between the NVA and VC were deep and complex. Even though the NVA was obtrusively "supporting" the NLF's war of liberation, there was little doubt the VC were secondary to the NVA. The NVA did rely on the VC to provide local intelligence on terrain, the civilian population, local government security units, Free World forces and their movements, trails, water points and other information. The VC also provided guides to NVA units passing through their area, prepared base camps and would lead NVA reconnaissance teams to scout Free World installations they planned to attack, and place surveillance on the enemy's patrol routes. The VC would also provide food and basic supplies. They would also arrange for porters and laborers from the local population, whose co-operation may have been voluntary or forced. Besides hauling supplies, weapons and ammunition, they built base camps and fortifications, made booby traps and set up punji stakes, installed camouflage, recovered and buried the dead, carried away captured materials from attacked Free World bases and so on.

North Vietnam began sending regular cadres to support the VC in the RVN in 1958. The next year it declared its "political struggle" was changed to an "armed struggle" and regular NVA troops began to be sent south. As the war escalated more units were sent south and it was not long before entire divisions and support troops were being deployed.

As early as 1964 NVA troops were being assigned to VC units to make up losses and provide a better-trained backbone. Military and political cadres – specially trained and selected leaders – were assigned to many VC units. The VC was virtually decimated, by North Vietnamese design, during the 1968 Tet Offensive. Many VC units remained drastically understrength or dwindled away as popular support deteriorated. They were often no longer able to recruit meaningful numbers from the civilian population. Selected units received NVA fillers, up to 90 percent strength, whilst still retaining their "VC" designations. VC-dominated units operated in the Mekong Delta, the RVN's extreme south, a region that saw very limited NVA presence until mid-1969.

The American soldier had a myriad of names for the VC: "Victor Charlie," "Charlie," "Charles," "Mr. or Sir Charles," "Chuck," or "the Cong." The NVA, in contrast, were simply the "NVA," or sometimes the redundant "NVA regulars." The Americans did apply general derogatory nicknames to them that were used for any Vietnamese, such as "gook," "dink," "slope," "slope-head," "zip," or "zipper-head." "Gook" was probably the most common disparaging nickname applied to the NVA or VC.

One often sees the term "VC/NVA" used as though they were one and the same. The VC were South Vietnamese communist insurgents fighting a guerrilla war against government forces and Free World forces. The NVA was, in its own way, a conventional army. It was as different from the VC as a professional army is from a locally raised, part-time militia.

The NVA was an extremely politicized force with political controls integrated into all echelons and aspects of the soldier's life. Soldiers (bo doi) were expected to be totally committed to the Revolution. They were expected to sacrifice all for the cause.

# CHRONOLOGY

By both policy and ingrained philosophy, the NVA focused on fighting the US Army and US Marines. They seldom demonstrated hesitation in engaging their main enemy, even when faced with superior firepower.

**1935**
August          Viet Minh formed. Revealed itself in May 1941.

**1945**
September 2     Ho Chi Minh declares the Democratic Republic of Vietnam at the end of World War II.

**1946**
December 19     First Indochina War between Vietnamese Communist forces with French Union forces.

**1955**
February 12     First US military advisors arrive in RVN.

July 21         Vietnam divided at the 17th Parallel as the French withdraw.

**1959**
January         DRV issues resolution changing its "political struggle" in RVN to an "armed struggle."

June            DRV begins developing the Ho Chi Minh Trail to RVN.

October         Communist Party and Viet Minh outlawed by RVN.

**1960**
December 20     National Liberation Front (VC) formed.

**1961**
May 5           US announces support troops will be deployed to RVN.

**1962**

January 1      People's Revolutionary Party established in RVN.

**1964**

August 2–4      US destroyers attacked by DRV torpedo boats in the Gulf of Tonkin.

August 7      US Congress passes Gulf of Tonkin Resolution to counter DRV aggression.

December      First NVA regiment deployed to RVN.

**1965**

February 7      US authorizes air attacks on DRV commencing February 24.

March 8      First US Marine ground combat troops arrive in RVN.

April 6      US ground troops authorized to conduct offensive operations. Publicly announced June 8.

May 7      First US Army conventional ground combat troops arrive in RVN.

**1966**

June      First full NVA division deployed to RVN.

October 25      US offers to withdraw all troops six months after DRV withdraws from RVN. Rejected by DRV.

**1968**

January 30      VC and NVA initiate Tet Offensive, which ends February 26 with heavy VC/NVA losses.

March 31      US announces de-escalation of its war effort and halts bombing of North Vietnam.

May 12      Peace talks begin in Paris.

September      "Mini Tet" Offensive launched by remaining VC is defeated.

**1969**

June 8      US initiates Vietnamization Program to turn the war effort over completely to RVN.

July 1      First US Army units commence withdrawal.

September 2      Ho Chi Minh dies.

**1970**

April 29      Free World offensive operations into Cambodia to neutralize NVA/VC sanctuaries.

## 1971

**August 18**    Last Australian and New Zealand troops withdraw.

## 1972

**March 30**    NVA Easter Offensive (Nguyen Hue campaign) commences, lasting most of the year.

## 1973

**January 15**    US announces halt of all offensive ground actions.

**January 27**    Ceasefire agreement is signed in Paris.

**March 29**    Last US troops withdraw.

## 1974

**December 13**    Ho Chi Minh campaign commences, planned to eventually defeat RVN by May 1, 1975.

## 1975

**March 10**    NVA Campaign 275 to seize the Central Highlands commences. ARVN crumbles and campaign goals are extended.

**April 30**    Saigon falls to NVA.

**Mid-May**    DRV officially makes it clear the NLF and PRA have no part in the new Vietnam.

## 1976

**July 2**    North and South Vietnam officially unified.

# ORGANIZATION

The NVA was an all-encompassing armed force; the air force and navy were components of the army alongside the much larger ground forces. NVA organization was rather nebulous with overlapping and inconsistent responsibilities. This was owing to intentional redundancies to ensure the survival of command structures, secrecy and the existence of warlord-like "fiefdoms." Reorganizations, activation of new commands and reassignments were frequent. Many senior commanders wore multiple "hats," being responsible for a number of commands and organizations.

Regionally the DRV divided North and South Vietnam into three regions: North (Buc Bo) with zones 1–3, Central (Trung Bo) with zones 4–6 and South (Nam Bo) with zones 7–9. These three regions coincided with the old French Union, separately administered colonies of Tonkin, Annan and Cochin China respectively. In 1965 the zones were redesignated military regions (*quan khu*). Zones 5–9 were in the RVN and comprised administrative control regions for NVA units in the South; they were under the control of the Central Office for the South (COSVN – *Trung Uong Cuc Mien Nam*) established in 1960.

Units were assigned cover designations, which changed frequently. Many of these would provide no indication of the unit's identity or type; for example, one NVA regiment carried the deceptive designation of "Garden Plot 9."

The soldiers of the NVA comprised youths. Here an equally youthful French Union Vietnamese paratrooper brings in a wounded Viet Minh fighter.

The NVA Main Force, with formations in both the North and South, comprised the main operating forces for both the defense of North Vietnam – the "national defense war" – and the liberation of the South. The Main Force was also referred to as the Permanent Force, Regular Force, or Full-time Military Force. These terms, like many other NVA organizational terms, differ mainly according to translation. There was no standard established translation of military terms. For example, the term *doan* means "group" and *don* "unit," but these terms could identify any echelon of unit by adding a prefix and might be used interchangeably – *tieu doan* (regiment), *trung doan* (battalion).

Another component of the NVA were the Paramilitary Forces, which consisted of a bewildering array of regional, district and local forces. These under-equipped and moderately trained part-time units supported the "national defense war." They were further supported by local self-defense militia units, mostly companies, based around factories, communes, villages and city precincts. In the event that the country was invaded, they would conduct a "local people's war" – guerrilla warfare. They also served as a means of incorporating the people into the national defense and government structure, imparting basic military training and providing a pool of registered men for conscription. It was often this militia that turned out to capture downed American aircrewmen.

Operational formations were usually formed to control forces committed to specific campaigns. These were usually designated "fronts," which roughly equated to corps, but their structure could consist of any number and type of units tailored for the mission and included service organizations to support the campaign. A dual military and political command structure was employed. To give one example, during the Khe Sanh siege the Route 9-Khe Sanh Military Command and Route 9-Khe Sanh Party Committee were established to control the operation. Such dual commands would usually be co-located and were seldom situated inside the RVN, but across the border in North Vietnam, Laos or Cambodia.

Divisions were the principal operating forces, but there were also numerous independent regiments and others. Divisions and their organic units might have the letters "B," "C," or "D" appended to unit designations indicating "cloned" divisions formed from the original unlettered division. This is very confusing to order of battle specialists, especially since even North Vietnamese documents sometimes omit the letters. 325C Division, for example, is the second division, bearing the same number, raised by its parent 325 Division. The component regiments and other units would bear the same letter indicator. Wartime intelligence often omitted the letter from component regiments.

A full-strength NVA infantry division (*su doan bo binh*) had 9,600 troops organized into three infantry regiments, an artillery battalion, occasionally a regiment, plus antiaircraft, engineer, signal and medical battalions and a transport company. In the South, artillery battalions were mostly armed with 82mm and 120mm mortars and possibly rockets (107mm, 122mm, 140mm), although most rocket units were non-divisional. Those in North Vietnam had conventional light artillery, as did the divisions after 1972 when more conventional mobile operations were conducted to defeat the South.

Infantry regiments featured about 2,500 troops and three 600-man battalions. Units were often understrength and battalions were considered combat capable with only 300 troops. Battalions organic to a regiment might be numbered 1 to 3, but often they were numbered in sequence within a division; for example, 324B Division was assigned the 90B Regiment (7, 8, 9 battalions), 803B Regiment (1, 2, 3 battalions) and 812B Regiment (4, 5, 6 battalions). Companies were numbered in sequence through battalions. Three companies were standard, but after losses a battalion might only field two until replacements arrived. Companies were organized into one weapons and three rifle platoons. The latter had three squads, each with a 7.62mm light machine gun, possibly an RPG-2 or 7 (B40, B41) antitank weapon and sometimes a captured M79 grenade launcher. The weapons platoon would have a few 7.62mm SGM machine guns, two to four 60mm Chinese mortars and sometimes a couple of 57mm recoilless rifles. There was no standard allocation of weapons.

Besides the three battalions, regiments typically had a number of supporting companies directly under regimental control. The recoilless rifle company had 8 to 12 weapons (Soviet 73mm, US or Chinese 75mm and/or US or Chinese 57mm). The mortar company could have 6 to 12 Soviet or Chinese 82mm or 120mm mortars. The antiaircraft company had 6 to 12 12.7mm DShKM38/46 machine guns. The signal company operated the regiment's radios and telephones, with teams attached to battalions and support companies as required. A small engineer company, not always present, mainly assisted with building base camps, field fortifications and obstacles and maintained trails. Another unit formed by some regiments was the transport company or platoon, which man-packed supplies or used transport bicycles on the way south. Once in South Vietnam it might be disbanded or employed to haul ammunition and/or heavy weapons. The medical company had limited capabilities and mainly served as an aid station. In base camp it would treat the ill and maintained a modest hospital for recovery. Female medics were sometimes assigned. Some regiments raised a reconnaissance and/or a sapper company or platoon. Sappers were assault commandos, but they often conducted reconnaissance and surveillance missions.

Regardless of organization tables, the manning and armament of NVA units varied considerably due to lengthy campaigning, the availability of weapons and manpower and how they were configured for specific operations. The term "organization tables" is used loosely. Organizational documents provided only vague guidelines and commanders had a great deal of latitude in the organization of their unit.

NVA formations and units were organized into subunits of three – that is, three fire and maneuver subunits – alongside various supporting subunits,

**ABOVE**

Ethnic North Vietnamese were often taller than South and Central Vietnamese. Here a rain-soaked North Vietnamese interpreter poses with the author, who is 6ft 4in. Most South Vietnamese troops would only reach the author's shoulder.

**ABOVE RIGHT**

The most numerous weapons employed by the NVA included (left to right): 7.62mm SKS carbine, 7.62mm AK-47 assault rifle, RPG-2 and RPG-7 antitank weapons and (bottom) the 7.62mm RPD light machine gun. The Chinese versions of all of these weapons were designated the Type 56, with the exception of the RPG-7 (Type 69).

the number and type depending on the echelon and type of unit. There were exceptions, for example regiments with two to five battalions. This system of "threes" was carried all the way down to the internal organization of squads. Squads typically consisted of three, three-man cells (*to ba nguoi*) – also called a three-participant cell (*to tam gia*) or a glue-welded cell (*to keo son*). One cell would be armed with a light machine gun and perhaps another with an RPG-2 or 7 antitank weapon. These would not properly be called machine-gun or antitank cells, merely cells. Often the squad leader was not a member of a cell, but this varied from unit to unit. The cell was a means of political

**NVA ammunition**

(a) The 14.5 x 114mm (the second number is the length of the case in millimeters) armor-piercing incendiary (API) round was used in the ZPU-1, 2 and 4 heavy antiaircraft machine guns.

(b) The 12.7 x 107mm, also an API round, was used in DShKM1938/48 antiaircraft machine guns.

(c) 7.62 x 54mm tracer for rifles and machine guns.

(d) 7.62 x 45mm for the Czechoslovak vz.52 rifle.

(e) 7.62 x 39mm API for AK-47 assault rifles and RPD machine guns.

(f) 7.62 x 25mm for submachine guns and pistols.

(g) For comparison and as used in captured weapons: US 5.56mm for M16A1 rifles and

(h) US 7.62mm for M14 rifles and M60 machine guns.

(a)  (b)  (c)  (d)  (e)  (f)  (g)  (h)

surveillance to ensure the troops stayed in line, as a means of sharing work and other duties in camp and as a tactical element. Weapon crews, while they might have more than three men, also served as cells. A larger crew for a heavy weapon might be divided into two cells.

# RECRUITMENT

Committed to an armed military and political struggle to "liberate" South Vietnam, the DRV strove for the total mobilization of its population and resources. The DRV's population of 18 million produced approximately 100,000 draft-age males each year. In 1966, as the US troop build-up in the south was under way, the NVA consisted of almost 500,000 personnel. Of these just under half were in the Main Forces, the rest being Paramilitary Forces. About 58,000 were deployed in the south, with some 10 percent assigned to VC units as cadres. The war continued to escalate and the VC bled themselves white during the 1968 Tet Offensive. That year it was estimated that 200,000 NVA were in the south, of which 66,000 were assigned to VC units. By now VC units were such only in name, being mostly led and filled by northerners.

Ho Chi Minh (1890–1969) – known as "Uncle Ho" – the president of the Democratic Republic of Vietnam. He was as much a "spiritual" leader of Vietnamese communism as he was a political leader.

The demand for troops was enormous. Besides the many combat units in the North and South, forces were deployed to Laos and Cambodia. Among these were huge support organizations maintaining the vast trail and logistics networks. Besides formations dedicated to the defense of the DRV, large numbers of antiaircraft and construction units were maintained, the latter to repair the transportation network. China claims to have contributed 230,000 men in its support of the DRV, mainly antiaircraft, construction and transport units. Even if the numbers were half this, China's contribution aided greatly in allowing the DRV to send more troops south.

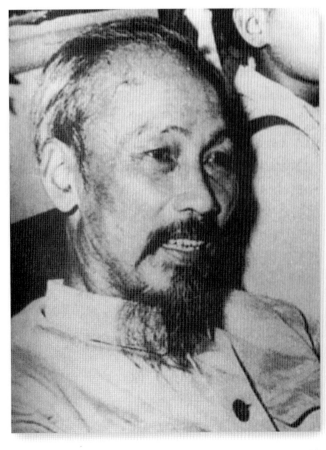

A young man's life in the North had little to recommend it, regardless of the national motto: "Independence, Freedom, Happiness." A typical house for a family of four to six had one or two rooms. Food was scarce and little variety was available in the cities. The countryside was little better and sometimes worse. There were many families who subsisted virtually on rice, *nuoc mam* (fermented fish sauce, a main source of protein) and vegetables. Cooking oil was provided by China and the USSR. The raising of livestock (pigs, chickens, ducks) was tightly controlled and animals were required to be sold to the government at minimal prices. Cooking was done on charcoal blazers or wood stoves. The cost of fuel meant hot water for bathing was almost unheard of, instead the

North Vietnamese would stand in a washtub pouring bowls of water over themselves. Water taps were located in streets and there were normally queues to use them; water was carried in 20- and 40-litre cans (approximately 5 and 10 gallons) on poles. Shopping was a lengthy ordeal owing to endless lines and everything was rationed. Medical care was socialized, but there was little to it. From 1965 modern medicines were almost impossible to obtain, except by the ruling party elite. Medicines from China and the USSR and medical personnel were sent south. For many, traditional medicine and home remedies were all that was available. This too was blamed on America and its puppets.

There was little in the way of entertainment. Television, watchable in community centers, aired nothing but government propaganda, government-controlled news and party-approved movies, often from China poorly dubbed or subtitled into Vietnamese. Government radio stations aired some popular or traditional music, but also a great deal of militaristic or propaganda-themed music, and of course much-slanted news. Announcements of VC/NVA victories in the south never mentioned their own casualties, only those of the enemy, which were exaggerated. Despite the threat of jail, foreign broadcasts were cautiously listened to: Radio Saigon, Voice of America and the BBC all broadcast in Vietnamese. School was conducted in shifts with morning and evening classes. Students did homework, and then worked in the fields or gardens the other half of the day. There was little to read beyond government newspapers, propaganda books and magazines like *Hoc Tap*, the Lao Dong Party magazine. Most students at 12 joined the Young Red Scarf League, having little choice. It consumed their "free" time with extracurricular actives from rehearsing dances, skits and singing performances, all with socialist themes, to organized athletics. At 16 they joined the Vanguard Youth and later the Young Communists League. The Party strove to control every aspect of personal life. The Three Delays (*Ba Khoan*) called on citizens to delay having children, getting married and even falling in love, as these were distractions to productivity. To complain or question was to be branded a defeatist or reactionary and those that did so were taken in for questioning by the police.

Except in the cities and larger towns, most private homes had no electricity. Power was cut off at night and there were severe blackout restrictions. Lighting was provided by oil lamps, which were expensive. Sunday was a rest day, but it was a day in which citizens were strongly encouraged to attend party

Young men of the Vanguard Youth, a paramilitary labor force of 16–30-year-olds, on their way to a work site to clear bomb damage. This served as a form of preparatory training for the NVA.

meetings and rallies. Children were turned out to clean the streets and young men and women dug drainage ditches and repaired roads. All national holidays fell on Sundays, leading to their being called "socialist Sundays." These were not days off, but a day of extra work with competition between factories and collectives. Certificated awards were presented, such as Hero of Production or Hero of Work, to individuals and enterprises, with the results announced in newspapers. Monetary or food awards were not given, as such material incentives were regarded as being too capitalist. Transportation was by bus and foot, and few owned bicycles; many had been confiscated for use as cargo bicycles on the Ho Chi Minh Trail.

In the cities and towns near military installations, air raids broke the monotony. PA systems would announce how far out the attackers were and then sound the alarm when they approached a target area. Older schoolboys often turned out to help with rescue efforts after the all-clear.

Military service was taught to be an honorable and highly esteemed means of serving the state. Regardless, there are stories of mothers who cried for days when finding out their son had volunteered or

Young girls also joined the Vanguard Youth and performed labor tasks. These girls are conducting a street patrol, one armed with a 7.62mm M1944 carbine. They reported traffic violations and the location of cluster bomblets and ensured blackout restrictions were followed.

was drafted. Between the 1st and 5th of January each year, all males who would turn 18 that year were required to register for conscription. This was not always complied with, or even known about by some living in remote rural areas, but district (country equivalent) military committee officials would make the rounds signing up young men to ensure their quotas were met. As the war wore on, the registration effort was improved. Able-bodied Class A males between the ages of 16 and 45 were liable for conscription, if necessary. However, only 18-year-olds and older were drafted, whilst few men over 30 were called up. Men with prior military service could be recalled, and were mainly used as instructors and in service units or administrative assignments. It was not uncommon for men to volunteer, encouraged by political announcements and rallies. Some were motivated by the American bombing as a means of fighting back. There were cases of 15–17-year-olds lying about their age. Formal birth certificates often did not exist. Some fooled recruiters, others were turned away, discouraged and even in tears.

Sometime after registering, young men were called in for physical checks. Many were deferred, either permanently (rarely) or temporarily and recalled each year for re-assessment. It might be years before they were re-assessed as fit for duty, which often depended on manpower needs as opposed to any real change in their physical fitness. Men in their late 20s and early 30s found themselves in this situation. The children of the former bourgeois class and those who had worked with the French were noted as being unsuitable for

A young NVA recruit armed with an AK-47 wearing the peaked field cap with an NVA badge. This cap was seldom seen in the South.

call-up, but this changed in late 1967 and 1968 when manpower shortages became acute. The undesirables suddenly found themselves accepted.

There were other, rarely granted exemptions from the draft. Among these were sole surviving son status, which was sometimes administratively ignored, education deferments for some university students depending on their area of study, those who were the principal support of the family – usually with disabled parents, senior party/government officials, skilled technicians and scientists – especially if involved in the war industry and volunteers in the Vanguard Youth. Students studying overseas were exempted and this proved to be a haven for the sons of many party and government officials.

The Vanguard Youth was a paramilitary labor force consisting of 16–30-year-olds, who often did not quite meet the physical requirements of the Main Force. Girls could join as well. A large percentage were from the bourgeois class, the sons of former landowners, landlords, factory owners and capitalists. They volunteered for three years' labor in the hope of redeeming their standing with the party, which was necessary to obtain a decent job. Others were drawn to promises of good jobs or the opportunity to study abroad in the future. The Vanguard Youth were mainly involved in clearing and repairing bomb damage and agricultural work. Some found the work too tedious, and, angered by the results they saw of the bombing, volunteered for the Main Force anyway. Being exposed to military discipline and hard labor made them ideal candidates for the Main Force and some found themselves drafted regardless of any exemptions, especially from 1972. Sometimes the excuse of disciplinary infractions was used for conscripting them into the Main Force. Many university students were drafted immediately upon graduation, and sent for officer training. There were, of course, no conscientious objector or divinity student exemptions. Medical personnel were highly prone to the draft, leading to a scarcity of doctors and other medical professionals in the North. Chinese medical personnel helped alleviate such shortages by working in hospitals and clinics. Young men who asked too many questions at political meetings or otherwise demonstrated less than desired socialist spirit were classified as reactionary or "halfway" elements. They were not drafted, being deemed untrustworthy, and were assigned factory or agricultural jobs.

Induction notices were usually received by mail, in the form of a letter ordering the conscript to report to a military base or nearby government center for a physical check. This was usually in December. In rural areas where formal procedures were not always practical, recruiting officials, usually accompanied by a few militiamen, did the rounds of villages, hamlets and farms. A conscript was handed their orders and escorted out of the rice paddy to gather a few authorized items and bid farewell to his family. Such a practice discouraged second thoughts, tardiness in reporting and speeded up the assembly of conscripts.

Following the Soviet pattern, conscripts and volunteers for the ground forces served two years, while the term was three years for the air force and four for the navy. In June 1965, with the escalation of the war, this changed. Induction was now for the war's duration and, if sent south, it was simply indefinite. For the new soldier, life as he had known it ended there, and he knew it would be a very long time before he would see his family and friends again, if ever. It was well known that if a man was sent south, it was unlikely that he would ever be seen again, and seldom if ever heard from.

North Vietnamese society became highly militarized. A multitude of organizations wore the uniform and distinctive sun helmet of the NVA.

# TRAINING

Assembled conscripts were transported by train, bus or truck to military bases, usually in their home military zone (not that the location mattered, as no leave was allowed). Their basic training, called "School of the Soldier" along Soviet lines, was generally 12 weeks in duration. Some troops underwent only eight weeks' training, especially if they were to receive additional specialist training. There were no options allowing recruits to request specific branches or training. They went through a categorization process, usually conducted at the province level and unknown to them. Uniforms and equipment were issued. Basic infantry training was included in this instruction regardless of what specialty training soldiers might receive later. The training might be conducted at a recruit training depot and then the troops assigned to a unit or sent to specialty training. Others were assigned directly to newly raised units or to units preparing to march south. They would undergo their basic training provided by the unit and then be assigned to subunits for on-the-job training.

Initially they learned military discipline, marching, saluting, field sanitation, camouflage, bayonet, rifle assembly and disassembly, use of hand grenades (using dummy grenades only), rifle marksmanship and sometimes familiarization firing with other infantry weapons, especially light machine guns. The amount of ammunition expended was limited. Rigorous physical conditioning as conducted by Western armies was minimal. Spread throughout the training program was the equivalent of two weeks of political indoctrination. Recruits had long been accustomed to government propaganda and motivational lectures provided in schools, workplaces, on the radio and in newspapers and magazines. All the effort of the individual was directed at supporting the revolution, which had brought freedom to the North and would do so in the South. Revolution and liberation were the bylines.

Instruction was by rote and repetition. Often platoons stood at attention in formation while being lectured. At other times they were allowed to squat during instruction. They would be lectured on how to complete specific tasks, with perhaps a demonstration provided, and then they practiced it over and over. The skills were simple. Those failing to successfully accomplish them were often required to continue their efforts after duty hours. There was little shouting and harsh treatment, in contrast to the experiences of recruits in most armies. Training was conducted six days a week and began soon after sunrise. Sundays were filled with political lectures, cleaning up, clothes washing, and so on.

Infantry skills were very basic, and not oriented to combat in the South. This was because experienced combat troops were never rotated back to the north and there was little effort to collect and pass on lessons learned at the troop level. Infantry training was limited only to squad-level movement formations, attack maneuvers, defensive tactics, camouflage measures, defense against air attack (returning fire with small arms), digging fighting positions and individual movement techniques. The latter involved a lot of crawling, rolling from cover to cover, shooting positions, etc. Infantrymen continued to undertake training once assigned to a unit. They learned to operate other weapons within their platoon. Tactical training progressed through squad, platoon, company and battalion levels. For the most part it was purely by the book, under ideal situations with few challenges and variations. There was no aggressive, unco-operative "enemy" force to maneuver against and blank ammunition was seldom available. Night tactical training was minimal and when offered was usually in the form of forced road marches. The NVA were focused on mobile combat (*danh van dong*) and that meant a dependence on rapid cross-country movement.

Those selected for specialty training were sent to technical schools or undertook training provided by their units. This training could last between

 **NVA RECRUITS UNDERGOING COMBAT TRAINING**

Infantry training was very basic and concentrated on individual skills: shooting from different positions, hand-grenade throwing, camouflage, simple squad tactics and individual movement techniques. The latter were heavily practiced, as shown here, with emphasis on keeping a low profile, making use of any available concealment, moving quietly and preparing to return fire immediately. On occasion such movement had to be rapid, but it was also emphasized that, when covertly approaching enemy positions, deliberate, patient and unhurried progress was essential. These recruits wear the older tan uniform, sun helmet and jungle shoes and carry 7.62mm Type 56 carbines, the Chinese version of the Soviet SKS. Note they do not wear web gear. The sun helmet's broad all-around brim severely restricted vision in the prone position and presented a distinctive silhouette. The corporal (*ha si*) wears the field cap and service jacket displaying his rank in the form of collar patches. He has chosen to wear sandals. The stick he carries is used as a pointer and not for punishment. Lack of attention, errors and indiscretions would be discussed during post-training assessment sessions.

two and nine months depending on the specialty. Radio operators undertook nine months' training, which included operation, radio procedures, antenna theory, Morse code and minor repairs. Heavy weapons training could last up to nine months, while medics received three to four months' training. Officer training lasted nine months, and could be followed by further specialty courses. Training aids were scarce and what little equipment and weapons were available were often in worn condition or obsolescent items rather than of frontline quality. There was little ammunition available. A common complaint from NVA defectors and prisoners was that the training had not adequately prepared them for warfare and conditions in the South. Generally, once units had arrived in the South and replacements had been assigned to existing units, recruits did receive some degree of more practical training from experienced cadres.

# APPEARANCE

This .30-cal. M1 carbine-armed, tan-uniformed Viet Minh soldier, posing beside a French soldier during truce talks, differed little in appearance from an NVA soldier fighting the Americans some 10 years later. His sun helmet features a plastic rain cover.

Physically, there was little difference between North and South Vietnamese. The average Vietnamese was 5ft 1in.–5ft 4in. (1.57–1.63m) tall and weighed 110–122 lb (50–55kg). South Vietnamese often claimed they could identify a North Vietnamese by physical appearance. Northerners were reputed to have more Chinese-like facial features, were taller, bigger-boned and had fairer complexions. While these features were slightly more prevalent among northerners, they were by no means widespread and could be found among southerners, albeit less frequently. Also, after the communist takeover, some 950,000 refugees fled the North to South Vietnam between 1954 and 1955. Most settled in the RVN's northern provinces or around Saigon. Their children were liable to be drafted into the ARVN.

It was sometimes reported that Chinese soldiers were found among NVA dead. This has never been confirmed. There was a large, long-established ethnic Chinese (*Han*) population in the North (fewer in the South). They were born and raised in Vietnam, had adopted the culture and spoke Vietnamese without an accent. They suffered little prejudice and were exempt from conscription. However, from about 1970, upon graduation from school, many were drafted into the NVA to fight in the South. The ethnic Chinese were typically taller and fairer skinned.

The one certain way to identify a North from a South Vietnamese was by language. There are three mutually comprehensible Vietnamese dialects: North, Central and South. Vietnamese is a tonal language and there is much variation in accents between

These girls, members of a village self-defense militia, work the fields armed with .30-cal. M1903 Springfield rifles in case they are called out to search for downed American flyers. These rifles may have been provided by China, as the Nationalist Chinese received them in World War II as part of the lend-lease program. Women from local populations in Laos, Cambodia and South Vietnam were pressed into serving as porters, mainly hauling locally produced rice "donated" to the cause.

the three dialects. The northern dialect is difficult for southerners to understand and many words and phrases are different. The equivalent to "you guys" in the northern dialect is *chúng mày*, in the central it is *bon bây* and in the south, *tui mày*. An American unschooled in Vietnamese hearing a North and a South Vietnamese converse would have no idea who was speaking which dialect or that they were even speaking different dialects. The Central dialect was found in both North and South Vietnam roughly stretching from Nghe An Province south to Quang Nam Province. Military and political terminology also differed between North and South Vietnam owing to Soviet and Chinese communist influence.

Few Vietnamese needed to shave, or did so very infrequently, and even then only on the chin and upper lip. The typical "NVA haircut" was longish on top and short on the sides and the nape of the neck, and would give away NVA attempting to pose as southerners. It was sometimes difficult to tell VC Main Forces from NVA, but generally the latter were better armed, equipped and uniformed. They were often better fed than the VC and tended to look more rugged. While it might be difficult to differentiate between an NVA soldier and VC Main Force fighter, a group of NVA soldiers often appeared more professional and ordered than their VC counterparts, and their uniforms and equipment looked more standardized and better maintained.

## Uniforms

Recruits arrived at the training depot wearing civilian clothes, which were then handed in. They were issued two sets of field uniforms of simple design not much different from those civilian workers wore. It was certainly not a case of the uniform making the man feel like a soldier – his combat equipment and a weapon accomplished that. While many uniforms were factory produced, they were also made in small shops and even at home by piecework using a standard design – loose fitting, one size fits all. They were also produced in China, the USSR and Bulgaria. The pleated breast pockets were closed by scalloped, buttoned flaps. The pocket pleats were not always present, especially in later shirt models. The collar was of the stand-and-fall type and the front was fastened by four plastic buttons, which may or may not have matched the uniform color. Cuffs might be straight or with a single button, especially officers' uniforms. The latter were of noticeably better quality and workmanship. The trousers had two front pockets, one or two hip pockets and a buttoned fly. Trousers were provided with belt loops and and sometimes button straps at the cuff.

The standard uniform color up to 1966 was darkish tan, often described as khaki. Shades varied depending on fabric lots and sometimes the shirts and trousers did not match. From 1966 green uniforms began to be issued to provide better camouflage in a vividly green country. This was a darker green than the olive green worn by US and ARVN troops. Again, shades varied and included light green and brownish olive drab. Tan uniforms continued to be worn until they wore out, and it was not uncommon for green and tan and other color uniform components to be mixed. Uniform colors faded considerably with washing and exposure to sunlight. It was not uncommon, for example, for a new green shirt to be worn with heavily faded trousers. Unless a unit had recently been re-outfitted in Laos or Cambodia its dress would be far from uniform in color. Nor were different-colored uniforms reserved for specific units, as sometimes suggested.

Other colors of uniforms were encountered, including medium blue, light gray or brown. These were worn by militia in the north and found their way to the south on former militiamen or to fulfill uniform requirements. Large numbers of them began appearing in the south after the 1968 Tet Offensive when more units were sent from the north. Purple uniforms were reported, but these may have been faded black or simply wet light brown uniforms. Black, blue and white South Vietnamese peasant clothing was worn in base camps and sometimes when conducting reconnaissance or traveling in the open; these are the outfits known to Americans as "pajamas" or "P.J.s." ARVN and US uniform components were sometimes worn, not for deception purposes but merely as replacements. The first live NVA soldier the author saw close up was a very co-operative prisoner dressed in an extremely worn out, oversized, US, four-color, woodlands camouflage shirt and faded olive green ARVN trousers.

A light cotton, dark green, waist-length jacket saw limited use in the South. In the North it was intended as a service jacket. It had breast pockets with flaps, a waistband and was closed by six buttons. An olive green or dark blue V-neck wool and cotton-blended sweater for cool weather in North Vietnam and the northern mountains of the south was provided. Green and gray sweatshirts were also used in cold weather.

Trouser belts were similar to the equipment belt, but narrower and with simplified buckles, with or without a star. Some soldiers painted the star red;

**B**  **RECRUIT UNIFORM AND EQUIPMENT, NORTH VIETNAM**
Even though the dark green uniform began to replace the tan one in the south in 1966, the tan and other colors remained in general use in the north. This infantry recruit (**1** and **2**) is outfitted with only an SKS 10-pocket ammunition belt and canteen. Both Chinese Type 56 (**3**) and Soviet SKS (**4**) carbines were used. The 10-pocket cartridge belt (**5**) held two 10-round charger clips (**6**) in each pocket. A cleaning kit was provided to each man in different types of pouches, here black artificial leather (**7**). The Ground Forces badge (**8**) was affixed to the front of the sun helmet (**9**), which had an adjustable plastic headband (**10**). Examples of two types of canteen carriers are shown here (**11**), as well as a semi-pointed entrenching tool (**12**). Rank insignia was worn only in the North. The following are enlisted insignia: private 2nd class – *binh nhi* (**13a**), private 1st class – *binh nhat* (**13b**), corporal – *ha si* (**13c**), sergeant – *trung si* (**13d**) and master sergeant – *thuong si* (**13e**).

11

7

12

5

9

10

8

6

1

2

4

3

13e

13d

13c

13b

13a

Government officials and their children often wore uniform in an effort to set an example.

they were not issued this way. The web belts might be light green, olive green or tan. China provided a brown artificial leather belt with a light web backing, which deteriorated quickly in tropical areas. It was rumored among US troops that leather belts were worn only by officers, but this is not true. Web cargo and seatbelt straps recovered from downed helicopters were also used as belts. Many men wore white or green loincloths, but were issued two pairs of boxer-style undershorts of various colors. Socks might be white, tan, green or other colors, although many did not wear them at all.

The standard footwear was a North Vietnamese or Chinese "jungle shoe" similar to the old French Pataugas jungle boots. They were similar to tennis shoes with light green, tan or (rarely) black canvas uppers and a black rubber sole and toe cap; Chinese-made shoes only came in green. The soles had zigzag or V- and crescent-shaped lugs. These shoes dried quickly when wet, but offered limited ankle support; however, most Vietnamese had grown up barefoot or wearing sandals so this presented few problems. The jungle shoes were far less durable than American footwear so replacements were constantly sought. Bata boots, similar to the jungle shoes, that were issued to the Special Forces-advised Civilian Irregular Defense Group were removed from any dead encountered and used by the NVA, as were US-style jungle boots worn by the ARVN.

Ho Chi Minh sandals, known as "tire sandals" (*dep vo xe*), featured truck-tire treads as soles and strips of inner tube for straps. These were extremely durable, and broken straps were easily replaced. Common rubber shower shoes ("flip-flops") – what the Vietnamese called "Japanese slippers" – and any other type of civilian sandals were worn, especially in camps.

A defining accessory of the NVA was the sun helmet made of compressed fiberboard covered with light green, olive green, tan or brown cloth. This led the NVA and VC Main Force to be called "hard hats" (*non coi*). There were two ventilation eyelets on either side and an adjustable headband and artificial leather chinstrap, often removed. When present the strap was secured over the front brim. While there was an eyelet in the front for attaching the NVA insignia (gold star on a red backing with a gold wreath border), this was very seldom worn in the south. Helmets were sometimes covered with the green plastic cut from rain capes. This helmet only served to protect from the sun and rain and offered no protection against ballistics. Soviet SSh-40 and SSh-60 steel helmets saw some use, mainly by antiaircraft crews.

Bush hats of the French design had a full brim and rounded crown. They were issued with a cloth-tape chinstrap, but this was often cut off and used for other purposes. As with uniforms these could be found in any color. A visored field cap was also issued, but saw little use in the South.

Long scarves were looped once around the neck as a sweat cloth. These could be of red, green, black and white checks, red and white stripes and other colors. Some units used a common color as a means of "friend or foe" recognition. Special Forces reconnaissance teams and long-range patrol teams were constantly on the prowl and, even when dressed differently from VC/NVA troops, were difficult to identify at a distance. Different-colored hats (mostly green and black) were worn on specific days for the same purpose. US, four-color camouflage, nylon parachute cloth scarves were also used. These were also used as a camouflage device cut square or rectangular with rounded corners. The upper corners were knotted on the chest and these worn over the shoulders, upper arms and the back to include the rucksack. Small camouflage nets were sometimes draped over the shoulders and back, and could be pulled over the head. As a unit moved each man would attach vegetation to the net on the man in front whenever the plant life changed. Netting was also attached to sun helmets.

Prior to 1958 no rank insignia was worn by the NVA. Duty positions were identified by their title (platoon commander, deputy company commander, etc.) along Chinese lines. Following the 1957 modernization of the NVA along the lines of the Soviet model, formal rank titles were adopted along with collar insignia for field and service uniforms and shoulder boards for dress uniforms. Insignia was almost never worn in the South in order to maintain the charade that only Southerners were fighting there and to deny intelligence information.

Bayonet training, a common aspect of recruit drill in all armies, taught aggressiveness and improved co-ordination and stamina. This recruit wears a white uniform, often issued to recruits and militia. His weapon is a Nationalist Chinese-made 7.92mm Chiang Kai Shek rifle, a copy of the German Mauser.

The NVA did have a prescribed dress uniform, but it was issued only to generals, senior officials and honor guards in the North. This was a Soviet-style, olive drab tunic and trousers with rank shoulder boards and branch insignia on the collars. A visored service cap was used, usually with a red cap band. Green, tan, white and other colored shirts were used along with black, green or brown neckties.

# WEAPONS AND EQUIPMENT

## Weapons

Before joining the military, few Vietnamese had gained experience of handling firearms, driving vehicles or operating powered farm machinery and mechanical or electronic equipment. Vietnam was largely an agrarian society, mostly producing food and rubber. There was very little manufacturing other than that of basic house wares, hand tools, farm implements and clothing. There was slightly more manufacturing in the North than the South, which was in the Hanoi–Haiphong area. This was a legacy of French rule, which had established some factories prior to World War II to support the colony. China later provided factories to produce ordnance.

Even with a poor education, especially among rural recruits, the Vietnamese soldier was a fast learner through rote instruction and repetition. Having often handled nothing more complex than a hoe, when assigned a modern assault rifle the soldier held the most complex and sophisticated device he had ever encountered.

Many soldiers had served in some paramilitary unit prior to being drafted into the Main Forces. They, at least, had had exposure to weapons, usually limited to World War II bolt-action rifles left by the French or Japanese or provided by China. The latter were usually in the form of further Japanese weapons plus pre-communist Chinese-made weapons, and an array of ordnance obtained before and during World War II from Belgium, Canada, Czechoslovakia, France, Germany, Great Britain, Switzerland, the US and other nations. China also manufactured licensed copies of some of these weapons prior to and during World War II. After World War II the USSR provided, either directly or through China, large quantities of its World War II weapons along with German ordnance.

Many of these weapons were worn through service. Spare parts were scarce or were obtained by cannibalizing unserviceable weapons. Spare magazines and machine-gun belts were in short supply. Ammunition supply was complicated by the 15-plus different small-arms calibers in use. It is often assumed that World War II-era US weapons had been captured in Korea. In reality it was lend-lease material provided by Nationalist Chinese forces during the war or that had been provided to the French.

The NVA Main Forces initially used the hodge-podge of weapons described above, but by the early 1960s they were being equipped with more

Many future NVA troops had served in the militia and as a result had basic experience of the use of weapons, drill and military discipline. It aided in keeping the School of the New Soldier limited in duration.

Recruits undergoing aircraft identification training. They were taught that any small arm was capable of downing even high-performance aircraft. Just below the poster is a Nationalist Chinese-made 7.92mm Type 26 light machine gun, a copy of the Czechoslovak vz.26.

standardized weaponry, especially those units heading South. The standard shoulder weapon was the Soviet-designed 7.62mm SKS carbine. The SKS was an ideal weapon for the NVA soldier. It was relatively light and short, a benefit because of their small stature, weighing 8.8 lb and measuring 40.16in. long. It was semi-automatic with a 10-round, non-detachable magazine. To load it the soldier fitted 10-round charger clips into clip guides with the bolt open. When the SKS was fired until empty, the bolt remained locked to the rear ready to accept the changer. The weapon was placed on safe, the rounds quickly pushed into the magazine by the thumb and the clip removed. The operating handle was pulled back and released, the safety lever pressed down and then the weapon was ready. Normally the changer clip was discarded, but NVA soldiers were taught to retain them. Ammunition was issued already clipped, but it was also often issued in bulk and packed loose. Retaining the clips allowed loose cartridges to be clipped whilst in camp.

Another favorable characteristic of the SKS was that the small 7.62 × 39mm round was the same as that used in the AK-47 assault rifle and RPD machine gun. It was shorter than most rifle/machine-gun rounds, and the low recoil generated made it comfortable for Vietnamese to use. The small intermediate round was not to be underestimated. It was not effective much over 300m, but seldom did the NVA require a longer range than this. The steel-cored bullet offered good penetration through brush, bamboo and typical cover materials. The SKS was fairly rugged, reliable and easy to operate and maintain. Most Soviet-made SKS carbines had a 12in. fixed, folding bayonet with a double-edged flat blade; early ones had a spike bayonet. Conversely, later Chinese-made models, the Type 56 (Chinese-made copies of Soviet weapons were designated with "Type" followed by the last two digits of the year adopted), had a 12in. folding spike bayonet, although early ones had the Soviet-style flat bayonet.

In 1967 NVA units in the South were withdrawn in phases to Cambodia and Laos where they exchanged their SKSs for Soviet AK-47 assault rifles. They were given extensive operator and maintenance training on the new weapons. Most were the Chinese-made Type 56 (not to be confused with the SKS). The AK-47 was a selective-fire weapon, easy to operate and maintain,

27

A government official reads a proclamation to troops early in the war as they prepare to march south.

rugged and highly reliable. It could be immersed in mud and water and was certain to fire without cleaning. The AK-47 used the same ammunition as the SKS, but was provided a 30-round magazine. The magazine could be loaded with the same 10-round charger clip as used with the SKS, but the magazine had to be removed from the weapon and a charger adapter fitted to the magazine. These were seldom available and the rounds had to be loaded singly and removed from the charger clips in the process. The AK-47 gave the NVA soldier an edge over Free World forces armed with 5.56mm M16A1 rifles and .30-cal. M2 carbines. It was heavy, though, at 9 lb 6oz (4.3kg) and with a full magazine it weighed 10 lb 9oz (4.9kg). Soviet and many Chinese-made models were provided a detachable blade-type bayonet (5.75in. blade, 11in. overall), but later Chinese weapons were fitted with a 12in. folding spike bayonet. There was also a folding stock version of the AK-47, but this saw only limited use. Later an improved version, the AKM, appeared. Using stampings, it was about a pound and a half lighter than the AK-47. Polish PMK, Bulgarian AMD and North Korean Type 58 versions were also provided to North Vietnam. Limited use was made of the Czechoslovak vz.58 assault rifle. Outwardly similar to the AK-47, it was mechanically different, but fired the same 7.62 × 39mm cartridge. The Czechoslovak vz.52 semi-automatic rifle saw even less use. It was chambered for the 7.62 × 45mm, unique to this rifle. The VC/NVA used captured M16A1 rifles and understood that it was lighter and fired faster (not always an advantage) than their AK-47. Regardless of all the positive feedback relating to the M16A1, the VC/NVA much preferred the more rugged and reliable AK-47 owing mainly to its better penetration. They conducted firing exercises to demonstrate this to their troops.

The exchanged SKSs were turned over to VC Main Force and NVA support units. Previously they had been armed with the Soviet Mosin-Nagant 7.62mm M1944 carbine, commonly known as the "K44" or "red stock" rifle; the Chinese designated it the Type 53. While compact and light with a weight of 8.9 lb (4kg) and length of 40in., it had a hard recoil. It fired a full-size, rimmed 7.62 × 54mm rifle/machine-gun cartridge and was loaded by a five-round charger clip inserted in clip guides with the bolt open. The permanently attached folding bayonet was a 12.25in. spike. Many service units retained it. A detachable grenade launcher could be fitted to the K44 and was known as the "AT44." Some units retained certain numbers of these to launch Chinese Type 64 copies of US M9A1 antitank grenades. These obsolescent grenades were of little use against armored fighting vehicles, but were barrage-fired against Free World installations.

With the SKS came the 7.62mm RPD light machine gun, the Chinese Type 56. More arrived with the AK-47. It was an excellent lightweight assault weapon firing the same short round as the SKS and AK-47. The 15 lb 6oz (7kg) RPD was fed by a 100-round, non-disintegrating, metallic-link belt coiled in a detachable drum. The belt actually consisted of two 50-round sections held together by a cartridge. When expended the first 50-round section would drop to the ground and had to be recovered before the firer moved on. The non-discardable belts had to be retained and reloaded with loose cartridges. This applied to other Soviet/Chinese machine guns. The bipod-mounted RPD, which could be fired from the shoulder like a rifle or from an underarm assault position, was 41in. long. It was simple to operate, easy to disassemble and light, making it a good assault weapon.

The $7.62 \times 39$mm short rounds for the SKS, AK-47 and RPD included special-purpose cartridges: tracer (green tip), armor-piercing incendiary (black tip, red band) and incendiary-tracer (red tip). It is often said that VC/NVA tracers were green while US tracers were red, which served to identify the source of fire. However, some tracer ammunition provided by China and other countries burned red. The VC/NVA also used captured US weapons with red tracers.

In the early days, wide use was made of two submachine guns. The French 9mm MaT-49 was an excellent weapon with a 32-round magazine, which could be unlatched and folded forward under the barrel. Together with its telescoping wire stock, it formed an easily concealed weapon. Some MaT-49s were rebarreled with a longer barrel to $7.62 \times 25$mm, the Soviet/Chinese submachine gun/pistol cartridge. Another submachine gun was the North Vietnamese 7.62mm K50, a much modified Chinese Type 50 (Soviet PPSh-41) with the barrel jacket shortened to lighten it and fitted with a Type 56 (AK-47) pistol grip and the MaT-49's telescoping stock with a 35-round magazine.

NVA troops on maneuvers in the North. They are armed with SKS carbines and have attached camouflaging vegetation to their rucksacks, a standard measure when traveling cross-country.

The PPSh-41/Type 50 with a 71-round drum or 35-round magazine, widely used by the Chinese, saw relatively little use by the NVA. These weapons were mostly passed on to the VC when the AK-47 became available.

A very valuable weapon was the Soviet RPG-2 antitank projector, what the Chinese called a Type 56. This "rocket propelled grenade" (RPG stands for *Reaktivnyi Protivotankovyi Granatomet* – rocket antitank grenade) is actually a recoilless gun; it has no rocket motor, but a propellant cartridge. This was a deadly weapon effective against most armored fighting vehicles, but it was just as valuable as a fire support weapon. The 85mm over-caliber high-explosive antitank (HEAT) warhead could penetrate up to 6ft of sandbags and forced Free World forces to erect chain-link fencing around bunkers to pre-detonate incoming rounds. A HEAT warhead is less than ideal for antipersonnel use as much of the blast is directed into the ground. Nonetheless, a PG-2 warhead detonation generated significant blast, fragmentation and secondary fragmentation. When barrage-fired upward to land in trees above enemy troops, the rounds would burst in the treetops and shower the enemy with blast, fragments and wood splinters. The RPG-2 weighed only 6 lb 4oz (2.8kg) and was 41in. long. A projectile with propellant charge weighed 4 lb (1.84kg). A propellant change was screwed onto the end of the tail boom and inserted in the muzzle of the 40mm barrel. The weapon was aimed using a simple iron sight and had an effective range of 150m against stationary targets.

In the South neither officers nor other ranks wore insignia, but officers could often be identified by the better quality of their uniforms. However, after lengthy service in the South they would end up wearing rank-and-file uniforms.

The NVA were issued a superior weapon at the end of 1967, which saw its first combat in the Khe Sanh area at the beginning of 1968. It was intended to be employed during the Tet Offensive. RPG-2s were turned over to the VC units. The RPG-7 (Chinese Type 67) was a heavier, more bulky weapon. It was also more complex using an optical sight, but it was easy to train gunners in its use. The RPG-7 offered increased range and improved accuracy, and was more lethal. It weighed 14 lb 8oz (6.6kg) and was 37.5in. long. The vastly improved, rocket-assisted PG-7V projectile weighed 4.8 lb (2.2kg) and was effective against stationary targets at a distance of up to 500m; the projectile would self-destruct at 930m. Besides ground targets, RPG-2s and 7s were fired at helicopters. North Vietnamese copies of the RPG-2 and 7 were called the B40 and B41, which the NVA often also called Soviet and Chinese-made models.

Hand grenades were extensively used by the NVA, including all types of captured US, French (in the early days), Soviet, Chinese and North Vietnamese models. In the South the VC provided locally manufactured grenades. One of the most common was the Chinese Type 59 stick grenade, which was also produced in North Vietnam. This grenade had its origins in 1933 and, while it was updated, it offered limited blast effect, poor

fragmentation (in an uneven pattern and often inflicting non-incapacitating wounds) and marginal reliability. It had a cast iron head, without any uniform fragmentation means, fitted to a wood handle. On the end of the handle was a screw cap, which when removed revealed a red sealed paper disc. Torn open, this retained a metal ring attached to a friction pull-cord activating a 4–5-second delay fuse. Another type of stick grenade with a slightly longer handle had a segmented egg-shaped head. There were also stick grenades with very short handles or either non-segmented cylindrical or segmented egg-shaped heads (designations are undetermined). Stick grenades were preferred by the small-statured Vietnamese as they could be thrown slightly farther than conventional grenades. Soviet/Chinese F-1 (Type 1), RG-42 (Type 42) and RGD-5 (Type 59) grenades were also used.

Crew-served weapons needed to be sufficiently light to be man-packed, in a disassembled mode. Mortars, for example, were disassembled with the tube, bipod and baseplate carried separately. Recoilless rifle barrels and mounts were transported separated. Heavy components such as barrels were slung on stout poles and carried by two or more men. The weight of ammunition was a problem, and a great deal was needed when attacking a Free World base. A porter could carry only three 82mm mortar rounds, two 75mm recoilless rifle rounds, or a single 120mm mortar round.

The Chinese type designations follow the Soviet designation. Company machine guns (*sung dai*) included Soviet 7.62 × 54mm DPM (Type 53), RP-46 (Type 58), SG-43 (Type 53) and SGM (Type 57) as well as captured US .30-cal. M1919A4 and M1919A6s and 7.62mm M60s. Soviet 12.7mm DShKM38/46 (Type 54) and US .50-cal. M2 machine guns were used by antiaircraft machine-gun companies.

"NVA regulars," as they were called by American troops, parade in their forest green uniforms armed with AK-47s. They were known as "hard hats" (*non coi*) after their distinctive helmets.

Mortars (*sung coi*) included the Chinese 60mm Types 31 and 63, US 60mm M2 and M19, French 60mm M1935, Soviet 82mm PM37 (Type 53), US 81mm M1, M29 and M29A1, French 81mm M1931 and Soviet 120mm HM43 (Type 55). 60mm mortars were generally found at company level, 82/81mm at battalion and 120mm at regiment and division levels. Mortars were the NVA's "artillery" in the South along with rockets.

Recoilless rifles (*Dai-bac Khong Ziat –* DKZ) were valuable for their direct fire against bunkers, buildings and vehicles. Most of these weapons used spin-stabilized HEAT projectiles and they were less effective than the fin-stabilized HEAT rounds used in the SPG-9 and Type 56. The US 57mm M18A1 and its Chinese copy, the Type 36, were popular as they could be carried by two men, one if necessary, and were accurate at a long range. The US 75mm M20 recoilless rifle and its Chinese copies, the Type 52 and the upgraded Type 56 (capable of firing fin-stabilized HEAT rounds), were also long-range, accurate weapons. The Soviet 73mm SPG-9 recoilless gun was a modern and effective weapon while the Soviet 82mm B-10 recoilless gun was a heavy burden to move and its accuracy suffered at all but short ranges.

The crew of an 82mm PM37 (Type 53) mortar prepares to fire a round from the Soviet-made weapon. They wear the early tan uniform and bush hats.

Rumors exist that the 12.7mm (called the ".51-cal." by Free World forces) machine gun and Chinese 60mm mortars (supposedly 61mm and sometimes called such by Free World forces) could fire US .50-cal. and 60mm ammunition, but the US weapons could not fire Soviet and Chinese ammunition. This is not true, ammunition was not interchangeable between either weapon. However, Chinese and US 60mm ammunition were interchangeable either way. The rumor is based on the fact that US 81mm mortar rounds could be fired in Soviet/Chinese 82mm mortars, but not vice versa.

The NVA soldier was provided quality weaponry for the most part. Post-World War II Soviet weapon designs were rugged, reliable and incorporated lessons learned in a very difficult war. Prisoner interrogation reports revealed few complaints other than occasional ammunition shortages. For most operations, though, significant ammunition stockpiles were accumulated and situated in multiple locations to accommodate resupply. They did not rely on captured weapons as their VC comrades, but nonetheless recovered and evacuated what they could. There might be a need for them in the future, they could be provided to the VC and if nothing else, denied to the enemy.

Common US small arms, including World War II weapons provided to the ARVN, were the .30-cal. M1 rifle, .30-cal. M1 and M2 carbines, .30-cal. M1918A2 automatic rifle (BAR), .45-cal. M3A1 submachine gun ("grease gun"), .45-cal. M1A1 submachine gun (Thompson) and 5.56mm M16A1

NVA troops training in the North. The collar rank insignia of the main figure denotes a private 1st class. He is armed with a 7.62mm PPSh-41 (Type 50) submachine gun, a weapon little seen in the South.

rifle. A common French-made rifle was the 7.5mm MAS-36, a bolt-action weapon with a five-round magazine. Even old pre-World War II 8mm Label rifles were encountered early on.

Pistols were little used other than as a sign of office for commanders. The most common was the Soviet 7.62 × 25mm Tokarev TT-33 (Type 51 and 54). The Soviet 9mm Makarov PM (Type 59) was extremely rare. It is often said that the Makarov was only issued to senior officers, but this was not always the case. Both pistols had eight-round magazines. Captured US .45-cal. M1911A1 pistols, what they called a 12mm, were valued prizes.

## Equipment

If one word is required to describe an NVA soldier's individual equipment, it is spartan. He traveled with the bare minimum of gear. His equipment was light, practical and functional, but only moderately durable and provided only the most basic amenities. Web equipment might be North Vietnamese or Chinese made. Occasionally Eastern European and Soviet items were issued, but usually mixed with Vietnamese and Chinese gear. US web gear, also captured from the ARVN, was used to some degree, usually out of necessity to replace lost gear. In the early days some use was made of French gear as well as former US World War II gear, which had been provided to the French.

Web gear was made of low-grade fabric and webbing. It seldom lasted more than a year in the harsh climate and hard field use. Most gear was light green of various shades, but tan, brown and olive drab were used. Metal fittings were a gray alloy, sometimes painted. Pouches and bags were secured by buttons, tie-tapes and wood toggles and fabric loops.

The issue belt was a simple light green web affair with a five-point star embossed, and an interlocking plain steel or nickel-plated brass or steel buckle. Ammunition pouches typically had belt loops on the back as well as shoulder straps. Often, though, they were not attached to the belt. This seemed to be according to individual preference.

Magazine pouches were made for AK-47 assault rifles (three, four or five magazines), K50 and PPSh-41 submachine guns (three magazines), PPSh-41 submachine guns (one drum) and the RPD machine gun (one drum). Two- and four-pocket grenade pouches of various designs were widely used.

This photograph of two NVA troops provides a good view of the AK-47 chest magazine pouch and rucksack. One man wears a black shirt. Mixed uniform components, with tan, green and black items, were common.

For the SKS carbine a 10-pocket waist belt was used with a pair of adjustable shoulder straps. Each pouch held two 10-round charger clips – 200 rounds. Sometimes an oiler or cleaning kit was carried in one of the end pouches. AK-47-armed men sometimes used this belt and had only two or three magazines, relying on a magazine changing adapter, and loaded the magazines with charger clips. Besides belt pouches, a Chinese-designed three-pocket chest pouch with a pair of adjustable shoulder straps and waist

 **INSIDE AN NVA RUCKSACK**

Whilst serving in Vietnam, the author had the opportunity to search a number of NVA rucksacks. The following is a typical list of the contents. Not shown are rations and personal papers, letters, etc.

1. Spare uniform
2. Spare undershorts
3. Ho Chi Minh sandals
4. Rain cape/hammock cover/groundsheet
5. Hammock
6. Mosquito net
7. Toothbrush, Chinese toothpaste, soap in plastic box and comb with cloth bag
8. Canteen, with seldom seen cup; the inscription reads "Born in the north to die in the south"
9. Cup
10. Rice bowl and chopsticks
11. Soup spoon
12. 1967 edition of Mao Tse-tung's *Little Red Book*
13. Cigarette packs and Zippo lighter
14. Field dressing
15. Weapon oil and solvent container
16. AK-47 (Type 56) cleaning kit (left to right – carrying tube that fits into butt plate trap, bore jag for cleaning patch, takedown punch and bore brush)
17. AK-47 magazine charging adapter

tie-tapes was provided for AK-47 magazines. This was widely used, becoming symbolic of the NVA. The magazines in the chest pouch actually provided a degree of protection from fragments and bullets. The author encountered a dead NVA, killed by multiple hits, but two 5.56mm rounds had struck the magazines in the pouch, shattering some cartridges (which seldom detonate under such circumstances). He would have survived if these had been the only hits.

The standard rucksack was a simple one-compartment backpack closed by a two-strap secured flap and drawstrings. Three small flapped cargo pockets secured by tie-tapes were fitted on each side and the back. Some had only two pockets. The adjustable shoulder straps were unpadded. There were long tie-tapes that were to be secured around the waist, but these were often cut off. Rucksacks were made of cotton canvas and varied from tan to dark green. See Plate C on page 35 for the typical contents of a rucksack.

Hammocks were cotton or nylon of many colors. Sometimes doubled rayon cargo parachute cloth was used – camouflage or olive drab. Plastic rain capes varied greatly in color too, but were usually some shade of green. Most were a simple rectangle or square sheet. Others had a slit in the center for the head and might have grommets around the edge, allowing them to be pitched as a rain cover over a hammock. Sheets lacking grommets simply had a knot tied in each corner to which tie-down cords were fastened. The sheet was used as a "blanket" in cool weather – it retained body heat. Some carried rolled-up fiber sleeping mats. Aluminum canteens, Chinese and North Vietnamese-made, were painted olive drab and had dark brown Bakelite screw-on caps. Plastic canteens were also used. It was not uncommon for names and slogans to be scratched on canteens along with simple soldier's art. The carriers were cloth pouches secured by two flaps, each with a small grommet for a tie-tape and belt loops fitted on the back. Five days' rice was carried in a plastic bag inside the rucksack or in a rice bag, a cloth tube worn horseshoe fashion over the shoulders.

All forms of Warsaw Pact and Chinese web gear, small equipment items (compasses, binoculars, first aid kits, etc.) were used. Pistol holsters were dark brown or reddish brown leather with a flap and an integral magazine pocket. Chinese and Soviet-made entrenching tools were important as troops constantly dug bunkers and fighting positions. Rice sickles, knives and short machetes were used to cut camouflage and clear vegetation.

# CONDITIONS OF SERVICE

Life in North Vietnam, whether in rural or urban areas, was difficult with few amenities and shortages in all areas. Recruits were used to hardship and doing without. On a brutal battlefield with a marginal logistical system, they adapted well. Conditions were extraordinarily harsh. The climate was an enemy to all combatants. It was hot and humid year round, whether it was the dry or wet season with their accompanying dust and mud and rain. In the North nights were chilly and damp. Fog and low cloud made navigation through the mountains and hills difficult. Mosquitoes carried malaria, dengue fever and yellow fever and there were occasional outbreaks of the black plague and cholera. Mosquitoes, dry land and water leeches, red and black ants, centipedes, scorpions, poisonous snakes and flies were a bother; most bit or stung or carried disease. Dysentery, diarrhea and "jungle fevers" were

Reconnaissance-commando (sapper) training took place in the South. Training in the North was rather superficial and "by the book," whereas in the South it was realistic and pragmatic in the face of Free World firepower and security measures.

debilitating. Heat exhaustion, dehydration, ringworm and beri-beri (vitamin deficiency) were common. Habitual dehydration led to thickened blood. When wounded and shocked, the blood vessels of an injured soldier would contract, and thickened blood complicated the problem. Beyond disease, many young soldiers suffered homesickness and longed to return home.

Barracks were either old French masonry troop quarters, or more often, wooden-framed structures with corrugated steel roofs or bamboo and thatch shelters. There was no running or hot water, and the latrines were outdoors. Cots or plywood sleeping platforms might have been available, but often hammocks were suspended between posts.

Some things were better than in civilian life, including medical attention and food. The regular daily NVA ration was .80 Dong while the average civilian ration was .60 Dong. Those preparing to go south were allotted 3.2 Dong to prepare them for the rigors of the trip and sustain them though their preparation training. Civilians were fortunate to have meat (fish, pork and chicken) once a week. Soldiers received some form of meat almost daily, albeit in small portions. Vegetables were also increased, but fruits were often limited.

Payday was at the end of the month and was minimal. Soldiers complained it was not enough to buy cigarettes; the majority smoked. In the North payment was in Dong. There was no official exchange rate with Western currencies, but a Dong was worth only pennies. A private received only 6 Dong and a sergeant twice that. If they had a family or non-working parents they received an allotment of 12 Dong if living in a rural area, 15 Dong in small towns and 18 Dong in cities, per month. Ration allowance was separate and may have gone directly to the unit or all or part to the individual if expected to live off the local economy. In the South pay was irregular and varied from area-to-area and between units, not because of authorized pay, but simply what was available. This usually paid only in the cross-border base areas, but troops were allotted what was called "spending money" to buy essentials in the local economy. This meant the South Vietnamese economy and troops were paid in RVN piasters. It is believed that the DRV counterfeited RVN piasters to supplement piasters collected in the South through civilian "war taxes" or through theft. A somewhat higher rate of pay was authorized in the South. Unit cadre personnel received as much as twice that of other personnel.

There was little resentment of this inequality as it was felt the cadre worked harder and had more responsibilities. Large quantities of DRV "liberation money" were captured by American troops found boxed in base camps. It was awaiting the day of liberation and was not used by the VC/NVA. It was of no real monetary value and American troops kept it as a novelty.

Troops bound for the South learned of it in many ways. Simple rumors alerted many and it was confirmed by the intensified training. In some units it was formally announced and in others the troops only figured it out after days of marching south.

## The path south

Units destined for the South began an intensive physical fitness regime. The quantity and quality of food was increased to aid them in raising their level of fitness and stamina. This was not just to prepare them for months of marching and then combat, but also to condition them for the rigors of the physical effort and make them more resilient to illness.

The main training focus was forced marches, day and night, carrying rucksacks filled with rocks, bricks, or sand on hilly roads and trails. Some marches were conducted cross-country on increasingly difficult terrain and of increasing duration. They would start with 10kg (22 lb) and work their way up to 30kg (66 lb). Daily marches were conducted from 9–11 a.m., 2–5 p.m. and 7–10 p.m. on some nights. Additional weapons firing practice might be provided. Little jungle survival training was conducted. Political indoctrination increased, spiced up with stories of victories in the South. Such training might last up to three months.

In rare cases some men were granted leave to return home. Some failed to return or deserted when informed of their fate. They were usually rounded up by the police at their home and sent to a re-education camp or often merely returned to their unit. Many were ridiculed by family and neighbors and even turned in. They were warned not to mention their deployment to locals or in letters to families. They were even discouraged to discuss it among themselves, although this was impossible to prevent.

Infiltration groups and units might stage through Vinh on North Vietnam's central coast, then to Dong Hoi on the coast above the DMZ. They were trucked to the Laotian border and sometimes into Laos. Seldom did they know when they had actually left the DRV. All letters, diaries and personal papers

**D** **THE PATH SOUTH**

Replacements infiltrating South Vietnam were organized into groups of between 5 and 500 men, but typically numbered between 40 and 50. Each man was issued a numbered infiltration pass with name and unit code. Troops usually received new uniforms and equipment plus may have been issued a new weapon, here AK-47s and an RPD light machine gun (both Chinese Type 56). They were also provided anti-malaria pills, antivenom, water purification tablets and lighter flints, but not antibiotics. While the trip could take up to six months, it typically lasted between one and three. The rate of movement might only be 6–12 miles (10–20km) a day, depending on the terrain, weather and the occasional American air attack, which actually had little direct effect on the troops marching south. Monsoon rains greatly lengthened the trip by transforming mountain streams into raging torrents, creating flash floods and flooding low areas, requiring lengthy by-pass maneuvers. Everything the *bo dai* needed was carried on his back, including a basic load of ammunition and rice for five days in their neck bags ("elephant intestines"). Once every five days they rested for a day and gathered new supplies. Carriers were seldom provided for entrenching tools and they were carried beneath rucksack flaps. Troops tended to wear the rucksack very low on the back.

This motorcycle courier is sporting low-topped running shoes; his trouser cuffs are buttoned to keep out dust.

were supposed to be turned in. They knew they were in Laos when they entered Techepone just south of the DMZ, the last vestige of civilization on the road south, the trail head of the Truong Son Road or Ho Chi Minh Trail. (The NVA called it Truong Son Road after the 1,500–8,000ft Laotian mountain range it traversed. The name "Ho Chi Minh Trail" was bestowed by the Americans, but the term was used by the North Vietnamese.) Units traveled south in battalion and company increments and would transport their own crew-served weapons with a minimum of ammunition. Replacements might travel in 5–500-man groups, designated a *doan* (group) – D-236, for example, with the leader carrying the group's orders. The most common groupings were of 40–50 men. They carried only individual weapons and a basic load of ammunition.

Besides the Ho Chi Minh Trail, some were infiltrated across the DMZ separating North and South Vietnam. This was fine for troops intended to operate in the RVN's northern provinces, but only exposed those going further south to an increased chance of detection. Smaller numbers were infiltrated by sea, but they too mostly landed in the northern provinces. These routes became increasingly dangerous.

Group 559 (*Doan 559*) was established to operate and maintain the trail along with thousands of impressed civilians. This 50,000-man command was organized into 15 logistical base units (*binh tram*), later 27, each responsible for 30–50 miles (50–80km) of trail. They typically were composed of two truck transport, engineer and air defense battalions each, plus one communications-liaison, signal, security and medical battalion each, sometimes an SA-2 missile battalion and a food production unit cultivating gardens and raising livestock. Besides defending, repairing, maintaining and expanding the trail system, the BTs operated way-stations (designated *tram*: T- followed by a number) and provided guides. Local Laotian and Cambodian guides were employed until 1965 when only VC/NVA communications-liaison agents (*giao-lieu*) were used for security purposes.

Infiltration groups were led by guides from way-station to way-station set at 6–12 mile (10–20km) intervals depending on terrain – a day's march. The pair of guides handed over the group to the next way-station's guides at a midway point. That way the guides only knew the location of their own way-station. The BTs improved trails, cleared mudslides and fallen trees, bridged streams, repaired bomb damage, built way-stations and even planted camouflaging vegetation in sparse areas. Resting posts were set along the trails, posts with two horizontal poles and a backrest on which soldiers rested their rucksacks without removing them.

Troops traveled on 2–4ft (0.6–1.2m)-wide footpaths, seldom on the roads. The trail was actually a vast network of interconnected, paralleling roads and trails providing alternate routes to bypass bomb damage, monsoon flooding, weather-hampered areas and to deceive American interdiction efforts. Some road sections were gravel topped, and saw improved bridges built and even fuel pipelines laid. Thousands of Soviet-made trucks hauled supplies, munitions, weapons and equipment south.

Way-stations were scattered collections of bamboo and thatch huts and lean-tos near a water source. Among them were bunkers and slit trenches for air raids. Every five days or so groups would take a rest day, depending on their physical condition. Rice was issued every few days and basic medical attention was available at some way-stations. Besides the high possibility of illness, foot and leg injuries were common owing to strain, rocks, roots, mud-slippery stream banks and hillsides. Drowning was common in rain-swollen streams.

Those too sick, injured or exhausted to continue were left at way-stations and when recovered, with little hope of treatment, joined another group. Thousands died en route.

Malaria was recurring, and afflicted individuals could relapse at any time leading to it being called the "jungle tax." It was contracted because of failure to take the pills, or because pill supplies were exhausted or were the wrong type for the strains in a particular area. Camps were set up away from the trails for the seriously ill, sometimes filled with hundreds of men in hammocks, from which the smell of death issued.

Other than rice, food was always in short supply. Primitive mountain tribesmen, who did not speak Vietnamese, traded food (monkey, dog, chicken, fish and fruit) for clothes, lighter flints, needles, knives and tools. This was an unreliable source though. The routine was to cook enough rice for breakfast and for a couple of lunch rice balls.

NVA soldiers saw the wounded and maimed in camps, and working at the way-stations and medical posts where they could still serve the revolution's goals. They heard horror stories, and saw

An 82mm PM37 mortar crew prepares to fire amid the ruins of Hue during the 1968 Tet Offensive, which destroyed large portions of the city.

the graves of soldiers, burned-out vehicle hulks and devastated countryside. The wounded were the worse part of it. They were missing legs and arms, sometimes both. Others had lost hands, one or both eyes, and were disfigured by burns or fragmentation wounds. Many were racked with malaria, dengue fever, or dysentery. Fed short rations and debilitated by their wounds and illness, they were skin and bones. Groups of 2 to 12 wounded would slowly walk home. The legless were carried in returning trucks. Many perished on the long struggle homewards, which could take months. Those who made it were wrecks.

Some en route to the South deserted. Heading for home was not an option, as they would be arrested there. Rejected by Laotians if they sought shelter in a village, hated by the Cambodians and fearful of attempting to go into South Vietnam, they lived in the jungle stealing from supply dumps and hunting and trading until they were caught or perished.

It took between one and six months to make their way south depending on the weather, American attacks and how far south they were destined. They could hear bombing and aircraft near the Vietnamese border, and the evidence of war increased. Infiltration groups began moving at night, and sleeping in the daytime. Fighter-bomber, Spectra gunship and B-52 bomber (from 1972) attacks battered the trail system. They learned about gravel bombs (*bomb bi*) – fragmentation bombs – and lake bombs (*bomb dia*), which blew huge craters that filled with water, used for bathing and drinking. Defoliants were sprayed and reconnaissance teams harassed infiltrators. Infiltration groups were sometimes turned out to hunt for such teams if they had been detected. The Americans even seeded rain clouds to extend the May to September wet season and dropped chemicals that destabilized the soil and created mud; neither experiment was successful. By 1969 the Americans had largely abandoned direct attacks on troop movements and concentrated on vehicle traffic to hamper logistics.

After finally reaching their destination, an established base area inside Cambodia, the groups were sent to assembly areas. It took weeks to assemble organized units as they trickled in. Replacement groups may have been assigned directly to an existing unit to replace losses. Others were broken up

An NVA veteran carries a bicycle across a log bridge. Its cargo of a few hundred pounds has already been offloaded and carried across by hand and will be reloaded on the other side. Horses and ponies were used to a limited extent to haul supplies on the trails. However, they were highly susceptible to disease and the harsh climate, required forage and actually carried less weight than a reinforced bicycle.

and parceled out to different units. Unless needed immediately for operations, they were allowed time to recover. They were thoroughly briefed on security requirements and welcomed to their new unit. Many found themselves retrained as mortar men, machine gunners, rocket crewmen and as other specialists. The NVA operated schools to train replacements. Mortar schools inside Cambodia conducted firing practice on Special Forces camps across the border. Extensive tactical training was provided infantrymen for the realities of combat in the South. This included individual and small-unit tactics, movement skills, camouflage, combat firing techniques, engaging helicopters and armored vehicles and building bunkers. This last was critical, given the impressive scale of Free World firepower. They learned how to construct and camouflage them quickly and to provide two openings to relieve blast overpressure. The NVA became used to digging ceaselessly (see Osprey Fortress 48, *Viet Cong and NVA Tunnels and Fortifications of the Vietnam War*).

## BELIEF AND BELONGING

A large percentage of the NVA were members of the Vietnam Workers' Party (*Dang Lao Dong Viet Nam*), the DRV communist party known simply as the *Lao Dong*. The party and government were indistinguishable. They strove to control every aspect of North Vietnamese life. All national and individual effort was to be directed to support the revolution. They were taught that it was their moral duty to free 15 million people in the South from slavery, and that to sacrifice some of their own people was unimportant in the context of achieving the final goal.

**ABOVE LEFT**
Camouflaged troops depart for the South through Laos. Morale would often be high at this point, but this waned as they pushed south owing to physical effort over difficult terrain, disease, illness, hunger, the brutal climate and American attacks.

**ABOVE**
Some of the Ho Chi Minh Trail's branches and spurs led across the most unlikely terrain, making it difficult for American reconnaissance teams to detect. Construction and maintenance required significant effort, as did traversing the route. In other areas, such as that shown here, the trail was totally exposed due to naturally sparse vegetation or defoliation by aerial-sprayed herbicides. Rest stops were interspaced along the foot trails, allowing soldiers to sit on bench seat logs. Besides crude foot trails the NVA also made use of metalled roads, which were often well maintained.

In 1954 the North was freed from 100 years of French colonization and a thousand years of Chinese slavery. There was an upwelling of patriotism; everyone supported the revolution and held a general hatred of colonialism and capitalism. The South, they were told, had been "invaded" by America.

Many soldiers sent to the South were not happy about this. It was common knowledge that once a man went south he did not return and was seldom, if ever, heard from, whether killed in action or by disease, illness or accident. They knew the trip was arduous and filled with hardships. They could not speak of it among themselves. Many of their fellow soldiers were willing to report any form of dissent. As a result, NVA conscripts held a rather fatalistic outlook. It was a challenge for the cadres to motivate and keep them motivated. One draftee conscripted in 1968 reported that over 100 young men had been drafted from his village since 1962, and none had returned. This fact was not hidden by the government. There was no return date, no specified time in service. Ho Chi Minh himself said, "Your duty is to fight for five years or even 10 or 20 years." Northerners assumed the South to be less developed and the people inferior; they viewed southerners as country bumpkins.

NVA soldiers were reassured that they would be welcomed as liberators in the South and that most of the countryside was under VC control. It was reported that the ARVN puppet troops would flee or surrender when the NVA appeared. The Americans were said to be heavily armed and vicious fighters, whilst at the same time were portrayed as cowards and mercenaries. The troops were told they would be tortured and murdered by Americans, that they were even cannibals. However, they were also told that the American people totally opposed the war and supported the communist revolution.

Viet Minh troops in the South in 1954 were told that victory had not been complete, and that they would have to accept a temporary partition of the country. Some chose to remain in the South to provide cadres for the political struggle. Others regrouped in the North to join the new army or do political work with the people. Those who regrouped were carried north aboard Soviet ships, while others crossed the new border on foot.

The first "NVA" troops of 301 Division sent to the South from 1960 were "regroupees." These were former South Vietnamese Viet Minh who were absorbed into the NVA. Unlike later troops sent south, most of the regroupees looked forward to returning to their homes and families – but this seldom occurred. These men were familiar with South Vietnam's customs, people and dialect. Some would be familiar with the area they would operate in, although much may have changed. In 1964 about 6,000 NVA were sent south and in 1969 over 100,000 more followed, the numbers increasing each year.

While the DRV Government denied the existence of troops in the South, it also stated that all were "volunteers." Some did volunteer, but the vast majority were ordered south once they had completed their training. There were propaganda rallies that inspired their motivation and masses of troops were filmed "volunteering," knowing they were going anyway. Troops were told that they need not concern themselves with politics, the party would handle that. They were to fight to further the goals of the party for the people.

Political indoctrination taught that the soldier was more important than the citizen; soldiers served to liberate their southern brothers from imperialist slavery and defeat the Americans, were part of the proletariat and were performing an honorable duty. The political cadres painted the most horrendous picture of

The entrance to a bomb shelter bunker in a trail rest camp. Note how heavily constructed the roof is, being made up of layers of logs and earth. There were always two entrances to relieve blast pressure. Bamboo benches and tables with a thatched roof shelter top the bunker.

suffering in the South. They told countless stories of the horrors and abuses, some based on fact, most fabricated or inflated and of course there was no mention of ceaseless VC/NVA atrocities against the people they were "liberating." The revolution gave citizens, now soldiers, the opportunity to actively participate in the class struggle to defeat imperialism and feudalism in the South. The ceaseless propaganda, lifelong indoctrination, inspiring stories of valor and enthusiasm of youth inspired even some of the more apathetic.

Even though the DRV was officially atheist, there were religious issues. The lives of villagers revolved around the veneration of ancestors and the anniversaries of their deaths, which involved rituals, feats and celebrations. All families participated in such celebrations of others and it gave villagers a sense of belonging. Catholics did not believe in some of the rituals and did not participate, opting to remember their ancestors in other ways. Buddhists took this as an insult. The few Catholics remaining in the North – thousands had relocated south in 1954 to flee communism – also suffered prejudice, as it was felt they were anti-communist. Many officials of the RVN Government and the higher educated classes were Catholics. From 1960 conflicts between Catholics and Buddhists broke out in the RVN, and the government crackdown against Buddhists only provided propaganda for the North. RVN President Ngo Dinh Diem was held in special contempt and accused of being an American puppet.

There was an unspoken feeling that the Americans could not be defeated. There was some resentment against party officials, even at lower levels, as most had not seen any combat. The army had local knowledge in the South, but party officials did not, and blindly accepted orders from the Central Committee without modifying them for local conditions.

NVA soldiers were subject to seemingly endless propaganda, which sought to motivate them to fight:

"Promote the mobilization of the people."

"Nothing is more valuable than independence and freedom."

"I follow only one party, the Vietnamese party."

"Remember, the storm is a good opportunity for the pine and the cypress to show their strength and their stability."

"For freedom you have to spend your blood."

"It is better to sacrifice everything than to live in slavery!"

"You can kill ten of our men for every one we kill of yours. But even at those odds, you will lose and we will win."

"Kill the wicked and destroy the oppressors."

An unofficial, but more cynically popular motto was, "Born in the North to die in the South" (*Trong the he Sinh Bac, Tu Nam*); this also appeared as a song and was frequently tattooed on the arm or chest of soldiers, or scratched onto canteens.

Regardless of the severity of the conditions, feelings of homesickness, difficult to believe propaganda and many other issues, overall NVA soldiers maintained a high state of morale and dedication to their mission. However, they were not natural "jungle fighters" as was so often claimed by Western media and even by US soldiers. City and town boys had no experience of the jungle environment and farm boys were little better off; they may have worked the fields, but they did not venture into forests. Most had an inordinate fear of snakes making movement at night a terrifying process – and so, if possible, they would use flashlights.

The B-52 bomber was a terrifying threat to the NVA soldier. There were instances when entire battalions were caught in bivouacs by the devastating rain of 500- and 1,000-pound bombs.

Many of the NVA high command and the Chinese felt they needed a division to fight a US battalion. Others held that the Americans could be fought one-on-one. The truth actually lay somewhere in between, but was highly dependent on the tactical situation, terrain and many other factors. NVA troops were taught to hate Americans, making it hard to understand why American soldiers had not been taught to hate them in return.

A dual-command system was operated down to company level, with a political commissar taking part in the decision-making process. The system had its flaws, but because of the extent of the Communist Party's integration into the armed forces and all aspects of North Vietnamese life, such an arrangement was essential. The deep mix of ideological integration, their unorthodox military education and development and the degree of their involvement in a lengthy, difficult war where self-sacrifice was an everyday occurrence shaped their nature. Officers were categorized as "careerists" (those emphasizing military skill and familiarity with military technology), or "devotees" (those devoted to and totally enmeshed in the party's cause).

Extensions of the Ho Chi Minh Trail reached into South Vietnam. These also possessed numerous branches and alternate routes. This one, being reconnoitered by American scout jeeps, is well camouflaged to prevent detection by aerial reconnaissance. Once in an area of operations NVA units made their own trails, which were very difficult to detect, even from the air.

# EXPERIENCE OF BATTLE

Whilst still in the North, typical NVA replacements would often walk for days from one base camp to another before reaching their new company, where they were welcomed and assigned to platoons. Some units made a small celebration of it. After major operations and the inevitable losses, squads had to be rebuilt and cells re-established. This came before all else, before the reconstituted unit commenced training.

While not considered an initiation (in a way it actually was), the new men underwent self-criticism along with the veterans. The recent infiltrators were expected to tell of their mistakes and the times when their will faltered during the trip south.

The new arrival found training in Cambodia different. In a way it was more informal, but practical. The instruction was obviously presented by men who had done exactly what they were teaching. There was no theory or rigid percepts here.

Anti-helicopter training was an example. It was apparent to the new arrivals that helicopters were something that veterans respected and even feared. They first learned the different types from a little newsprint booklet of poor quality photographs. The most dangerous was the "skinny helicopter," the *Kobra*. There were others almost as dangerous and difficult to tell from a distance from helicopters just carrying American or puppet troops.

A veteran with artistic talent sketched silhouettes of the different helicopters on the back of puppet government propaganda posters and these were pinned to the walls of a hut. A cadre member pointed out the vulnerable points on each type – the engine, fuel tanks, pilots' compartment, door gunners. They were taught how far ahead of the helicopter they were to aim allowing for its speed, range and angle of approach. The next step was for cardboard silhouettes attached to a cord strung between trees to be pulled

NVA assault tactics used little in the way of fire and maneuver. The assault would be preceded by mortar, recoilless rifle, rocket and machine-gun fire as well as infiltration by sappers. The assault would comprise a suicidal rush with some troops providing covering fire, as shown here from an AK-47 and an RPD.

across a clearing for non-firing lead practice. They were cautioned not to fire on helicopters unless they were obviously going to attack or were landing to deliver or pick up troops.

The replacements were surprised to learn they were assigned to the 9th Division, officially a VC formation, and were equally surprised that well over half its strength consisted of NVA troops, even more than this in their 272 Regiment. The division had taken a beating during the combined US and ARVN Operation *Junction City* lasting from February to May 1967.

No one knew how many men the battalion had lost, but the then 102-man company had lost 16 dead and 22 wounded. Five of those who died had perished from combat wounds. Almost a third of the wounded had not returned to the company. With the replacements the company now numbered 118 and a weapons platoon was raised with two 60mm mortars and a 57mm rifle.

RPG-2 and 7 antitank weapons were excellent fire support weapons for the assault. They would be directed mainly at perimeter bunkers and other defensive positions and fired at a high rate. This RPG-2 gunner wears a parachute-cloth camouflage cape.

Hue, 1968. Despite being trained only in jungle warfare, the NVA proved difficult to dislodge from buildings in South Vietnam's second-largest city. Here they have blasted openings in the internal walls of this building, allowing them to maneuver between rooms.

The battles were spoken of in whispers. The cadre did not like them to be discussed as to do so might be construed defeatist. Little was actually known about the company's history. There were perhaps six cadre and soldiers who had been in the company for about two years, during which the battalion had fought five battles. This gave an uncomfortable idea of one's life expectancy. NVA units often only conducted between one and three operations a year and actually saw less action than American units, who spent most of their time in the field.

Base camp life was rather relaxed in spite of training and endless work details. The day began at 5:00 a.m. with a stand to, cooking, breakfast and clean up. Training began at 7:00 a.m. and might consist of weapons or tactics practice, political study and constructing bunkers and fighting positions. The troops rested and had a light lunch from 11:30 a.m. to 1:30 a.m. in the

NVA troops overrun an ARVN airbase, where rocket-armed Huey helicopters are still parked, in what is probably a staged scene. The helicopters rest on their tails, which is not normal and there is other obvious damage.

day's heat. More training followed until 6:30 p.m., usually of a lighter nature due to the afternoon heat. Supper followed with a one-hour break. Training resumed from 8:00 p.m. to 10:00 p.m., often construction tasks. Guards were also posted and security patrols were conducted continuously. There were many work details, such as assisting cooks, camp clean up, digging latrines, hauling water, refreshing camouflage and being sent to the battalion camp to pick up rations, supplies and ammunition. Companies established their own secret supply caches, fearing enemy action and weather would disrupt regular supplies.

Patrols would visit local Cambodian villages, and there were crossroads at which merchants sold food, soap, cigarettes, lighter flints, utensils, batteries and other basics. The company combined part of the pay and food allowance of its men to make purchases. The ad hoc markets were awash with Cambodian, Vietnamese, Chinese and Laotian merchants, local shoppers and prostitutes. There have been reports of NVA prostitution units, recruited locally, but this has never been verified and was counter to the party's puritan stance. Although seriously condemned, some NVA female medical personnel and VC females ran their own prostitution rings.

One day the company commander accompanied a patrol to the battalion camp and they returned without him. He returned with a ration detail three days later and immediately called the deputy and platoon commanders. They talked for hours occasionally calling in certain veteran squad commanders. The next day 3 Platoon was sent to a low hill 1.25 miles (2km) away and began constructing three two-man bunkers connected by zigzag trenches according to a sketch. One veteran said these were like American bunkers. The next day 2 Platoon joined them and began planting posts in front of the bunker pits and

Loc Ninh Special Forces Camp and the district government center near the photograph's top; the town lies in the upper right corner. The fire support base is in the lower right at the end of the airstrip. It was across this airstrip that 272 Regiment launched their assault.

cutting hundreds of meters of vines to use as simulated barbed wire. They reported that 1 Platoon was building a model of a Special Forces camp and that their weapons platoon had been sent off, probably for more training.

Four days later the bunkers and "wire" were completed. The *bo doi* were surprised at how light the barriers were. There was only a 6.5ft (2m)-high, seven-strand, barbed-wire fence with two stacked coils of concertina and in front of the trenches two more coils. It was explained that the wood posts represented steel pickets and that there was tanglefoot tripwire and Claymore mines between the outer fence and the inner barrier. They were also told to ignore all the trees, though sparse here. Then it was said that the reason the barriers were so light was because beyond the outer fence there was an airstrip runway. The veterans were unhappy with the prospect of crossing almost 100m of bare ground and gravel runway under fire right into Claymores, and they explained what Claymores were and what they did.

During a unit meeting veterans questioned the feasibility of attacking across the runway. The cadre explained that there were fewer machine guns covering the airstrip side of the camp and that an attack would be unexpected there. The other side, facing the rubber plantation had four times the amount of barbed wire and twice as many machine guns.

They practiced a silent approach through the forest and then crossed the area marked as the airstrip, ignoring the trees. Each squad moved as a group in a stooped-over position and in step. This prevented an irregular bobbing effect among the body of men and would be less likely to attract the eye. They were taught to be absolutely silent. No commands would be given as they would do everything in practiced sequence. They were told and rehearsed on what to do in response to enemy actions. If they heard a mortar fire it was probably an illumination flare and they would lie flat and remain still with eyes closed to preserve their night vision. The same would happen with the pop of a trip flare. They would immediately begin moving when the flare burned out. If they were challenged by a sentry they would halt and not move for at least a minute. If there was no further response they would continue moving. If rifle or machine-gun fire opened up they would immediately launch their attack.

In contrast to usual practice, sappers would not go ahead to cut lanes through the wire. Instead, designated squads would cross first and emplace DH-10 command-detonated horizontal blast and fragmentation mines, circular equivalents to US Claymores. The DH-10 would blast a 13–16ft (4–5m)-wide gap though wire. They would also use expedient bangalore torpedoes. When the mines were detonated the rest of the company would rush across the airstrip. Those setting the mines would already be rushing though the gaps with satchel charges and grenades to attack the perimeter bunkers. Some men would carry scaling ladders.

They practiced day and night, with each platoon doing the other platoons' missions so that any one could be substituted for the other. Every man was able to set up and detonate DH-10s and bangalores. The three-man cells were used for this, with two men carrying the mines or bangalores; the electrical firing wires were already attached to the detonating devices carried by the third man who remained to the rear. Each man practiced being a carrier and firer.

The troops practiced while carrying the equipment they would wear in the assault: an AK-47 with three spare magazines, four stick grenades, canteen and two field dressings. Some men carried wire-cutters to clear unbroken strands, some shovels and others rucksacks full of ammunition cartons and grenades. Everything else would be left in their rucksacks in a hidden site.

Each platoon had its assignment and they talked and walked through it countless times on the model in their base camp. While they practiced breaching the wire time after time, they did not practice what they would do once inside. They knew what each building was. No subunits were designated to attack specific buildings. The veterans knew casualties would be high, there would be utter confusion among themselves as well as the defenders and they would be blinded and dazzled by muzzle flashes, explosions and flares. They were told simply to attack whichever key building they were nearest to, especially the communications bunker, American and Vietnamese Special Forces quarters, mortar pits and ammunition bunkers and to simply shoot at any movement in front of them.

## Into South Vietnam

After weeks of preparation the rehearsals ceased. The troops now endured boring days of political and motivational lectures. Supplies of rice, canned fish and ammunition arrived. They knew they would be leaving soon for enslaved South Vietnam. They were to say absolutely nothing of their mission to civilians and non-unit VC they would meet and not even to other companies. They were not even to speak of the mission among themselves unless a cadre was present and in the course of mission preparation.

**INFANTRYMAN'S UNIFORM AND EQUIPMENT, SOUTH VIETNAM**

The dark green uniform was widely worn, but tan and other colors were common. This infantryman (**1** and **2**) is outfitted to conduct an assault on a Free World firebase. His scarf is made from US cargo parachute cloth and can be used as a camouflage cape by knotting it around the neck and draping it over his back. He is armed with a Chinese Type 56 (AK-47) assault rifle (**3**). His equipment includes a web belt similar to the US pistol belt (**4**) and a Chinese-made three-pocket AK magazine chest pouch (**5**). The chest pouch had three one-magazine pockets and two smaller pockets on both end flaps that wrapped around the torso sides. The small pockets held an oil/solvent container, magazine charging adapter and cartridges in 10-round clips or cartons. Other available equipment comprises a Chinese-made five-pocket magazine pouch (**6**), Chinese-made plastic canteen (**7a**, widely used late in the war and carried in a pouch-like carrier) and an old type aluminum canteen with web carrier (**7b**), four types of stick hand grenades (**8**, designations unknown except **8a** which is a Type 59), four-pocket grenade pouch (**9**), Chinese 7 x 50 binoculars (**10**), Soviet compass (**11**) and sun helmet with a rain cover cut from a plastic sheet and camouflage net, with camouflage parachute cloth bows tied to it (**12**).

7a

7b

9

6

5

12

1

4

2

8a

8

3

11

10

After a hot breakfast they set out after first light. They had expected to join a vast column of troops, but it was two days of marching down jungle trails before they reached an assembly area. They were aware of couriers darting down trails and security patrols were seen. They rested the next day and were told from this point on they would move only at night.

Some of the march was on roads with wide intervals between units, and then they broke off onto trails led by VC guides. They walked from sunset to two hours before sunrise. There was a short break every hour and an hour break around midnight when they ate rice balls and napped. Entering their day's campsite they dug slit trenches and camouflaged them. A detail cooked rice, and after eating and posting sentries they slept. It was difficult at first because of the reversal of day and night. Sentries were changed hourly. In the heat of midday they had another meal. Water details were sent out, weapons and gear cleaned and more naps were taken through the afternoon. Supper was prepared and eaten with canned fish as the sun set. Rice balls for the coming night's march were passed out. Slit trenches were filled and they were on the march again. They never knew when they actually entered South Vietnam, but helicopters began to be seen and heard. It was early October 1967.

They established a base camp deep in the forest and there was to be no contact with civilians. There were rumors of agents giving the enemy their plans. They gradually learned what was happening around them. Their regiment and 273 Regiment were somewhere north of Loc Ninh Special Forces Camp and the district government center by the same name. To the south of the camp was 271 Regiment. A couple of weeks after their arrival a battle was reported to the south. Rumors said 271 Regiment had been discovered by the Americans and defeated, with the regiment pulled back to Cambodia after heavy losses. Their company marched for a night and prepared a new camp with increased emphasis on camouflage and security patrols. Porters delivered more ammunition, some of which was hidden in caches closer to the objective. Another model of the camp was built

Any assault on a Free World base was devastating to the attacking NVA units, even if successful (which was rare). Casualties of 50 percent or higher were common.

and each platoon went over its mission. The camp was defended by at least 500 Cambodians, Vietnamese, Montaganards and Chinese Nungs advised by about 10 Americans.

## Assault on the camp

Late in the afternoon on the 28th, the order was given to move out after sunset. Each man was given nine rice balls and four cans of fish and then filled their rice bags. They moved cross-country in single file, hanging on to the rucksack of the man in front in absolute silence. They found themselves 1.8 miles (3km) northeast of the camp at midnight. Shortly after 1 a.m. the sky to the southwest lit up with heavy mortar detonations and flares. 273 Regiment was attacking Loc Ninh District Town from the west. Then the camp began to be mortared. It was not long before flare ships and gunships arrived to light up the sky and send streams of tracer into the trees. They expected the attack order to come at any moment, but less than two hours later the thundering fire slackened. It continued sporadically until before dawn and then it grew quiet. Scores of helicopters filled the sky at dawn and it was thought reinforcements were being flown into the camp. Later in the morning firing could be heard from the town. The recruits had no idea of what was going on.

There were sharp firefights all day and more helicopters arrived. Word spread that more Americans were being lifted in and were attempting to box them in. There was also speculation that the attack on the camp was delayed to make the enemy believe they had withdrawn. They lay hidden all day. After

**ABOVE LEFT**
Aid stations were set up in advance of a major assault, not just in the vicinity of the objective, but along the routes back to Cambodia. This swampy surgical station is shaded by a parachute canopy, with mosquito nets providing the side walls.

**ABOVE**
During a major assault, casualties were heavy and the numbers of wounded were staggering. This contraption, comprising two hand-pushed bicycles and horizontal poles bearing two hammocks, also has a pair of seats on both the bicycles allowing four sitting wounded to be transported too.

dark two battalions of 272 Regiment advanced toward the camp and town, and mortars and recoilless rifles were moved into position.

2 Platoon was on the edge of the airstrip peering from the trees at the darkened camp. The men knew that an American firebase had been established at the southwest end of the runway. The tension was almost unbearable. There were flares drifting over the town, but the camp was quiet. They clutched their weapons wondering what would happen, how they would perform, if they would honor their unit and the revolution. Word was passed to prepare.

On order each squad rose and stepped through the trees, with the men crouching. Each of the three cells carrying their DH-10s stepped as quietly as possible on the hard-packed gravel runway then crossed the road. They reached the wire barrier and emplaced the mines a few yards from it. An occasional "tink" or rustling sound increased their apprehension. With equal caution they crept back to where the third man waited with the firing devices. Other cells were still crossing back when the thumps of their mortars firing began to be heard.

NVA troops undergoing a political indoctrination lecture in North Vietnam in 1972. They wear new dark green uniforms, collar rank insignia, and Soviet steel helmets, and are armed with AK-47 (Type 56) assault rifles.

 **LAUNCHING THE ATTACK**

A cell of three *bo doi* cross the road running parallel to the Loc Ninh Special Forces Camp perimeter wire to emplace two DH-10 directional mines (Soviet designation was MON-100). While it could be used as a Claymore antipersonnel mine and often attached to trees along trails, it was frequently set up on its issue tripod and used to blast gaps through barbed-wire entanglements with 450 steel 10 x 10mm rod fragments backed by 1.79kg of TNT. The third man would drop back with the firing devices, which are connected to the mines by electrical cords. They carry only their assault rifles, four hand grenades and canteens. Most are bareheaded; sun helmets and jungle hats would only restrict vision and even hearing, plus offer a more distinctive silhouette. Their faces and hands are blackened by charcoal. Beyond them is another cell carrying a scaling ladder and wire-cutters. The ladder could be used to bridge wire; it was shoved under concertina wire and then the outer end lifted about 18in. and propped up with Y-shaped sticks. Then a man would crawl under, lifting up the far end and propping it up to create a "tunnel" for the others to follow through. The ladders were also used to carry away any dead and wounded. The assault parties would move in unison to reduce the chance of detection.

Using local vegetation for camouflage, this sun-helmeted soldier sights an RPG-2 (Type 56) antitank weapon.

The pop of mortars from inside the camp immediately answered, and the mines began detonating with blinding flashes. Momentary silhouettes of *bo doi* still emplacing mines were seen as others were rushing across the runway with bangalores. Parachute-suspended flares burst overhead shedding yellow-white light. Mortar rounds detonated through the camp in white flashes. The clatter of machine guns erupted all around the camp, spewing out red tracer fire. The sharp cracks of recoilless rifles were highlighted by blazing backblasts among the rubber trees. Whistles shrilled, "*Danh tu!*" ("Attack!"). Every man was up and running creating tumbling shadows cast by the

This 7.62mm SGM heavy machine gun crew have camouflaged their sun helmets with camouflage-pattern parachute fabric secured in the netting. The ammunition container held a 250-round, non-disintegrating, metallic link belt. The antiaircraft ring sight is fitted to the gun, but this could also be used against ground targets.

A 7.62mm SGM crew provides covering fire in a posed photo (there are no cartridges in the belt). These heavy machine guns were mainly used as company support weapons. A lighter conventional tripod mount was also available.

drifting flares. Streams of green tracers swept into camp from the trees. Men tumbled, staggered and fell. Others were simply knocked flat like limp dolls.

The mines had torn broad gaps through the wire. Some trip flares had been ignited by the mine blasts, blinding white sparking glares. They did not pause in their headlong rush even though they felt completely exposed and men were dropping all around. Enemy mortar rounds were bursting on the runway spraying steel and gravel. Something did not look right. They realized the small bunkers and trenches were not at ground level as in their mock-up. They were dug-in atop a 6.5ft (2m)-high berm fronted by concertina wire. Claymore mines detonated in blue-white flashes scything through the *bo doi* like cut grass.

Two batteries of 105mm howitzers at the firebase on the end of the runway were firing volleys of high-explosive, air burst rounds straight down the strip, blasting apart the attack. Gunships and attack helicopters poured machine guns and rockets into the trees. The attack dissolved.

Some subunits hung on until 9:00 a.m., but most began a confused withdrawal before sunrise. Efforts were under way to recover their wounded and as many dead as possible, along with valuable weapons and equipment, to deny the enemy knowledge of the extent of their losses. Wounded were carried off on scaling ladders, and some of the dead were dragged along by ropes and hooks. A total of 110 men lay dead, left behind in the wire and on the airstrip. Camp defender casualties were very light and no NVA had breached the perimeter. Sporadic contacts were continued around Loc Ninh for two days as the NVA attempted to recover dead and equipment. American battalions had been inserted along the Cambodian border to intercept the reeling 9 Division as it made its way back. Over 1,100 VC/NVA were killed in exchange for a few score Free World casualties. (For further details on the Battle of Loc Ninh, see Osprey Fortress 33: *Special Forces Camps in Vietnam 1961–70*.)

The final victory, 1975. Victorious NVA troops in an overrun ARVN fire support base. The NVA were particularly disdainful of their ARVN enemies who "hid in bunkers like rats," in contrast to their assaults across open ground and through barbed wire.

# THE AFTERMATH OF BATTLE

Word of a soldier's death or serious wounding was sometimes passed on to families by friends who managed to return from the South, although these were precious few in number. Parents seeking information from the authorities drew a visit from the police. One simply did not talk about casualties in the South, and many never again heard from their sons. If a family did covertly receive word of a loved one's death, they could not publicly mourn.

It is often said that those wounded in the South remained in Cambodia and Laos. Many did, such as those able to work in supply depots, repair weapons and equipment, drive trucks, perform medical duties, serve as instructors, and the like. The more seriously wounded, amputees (prosthetics were unavailable), those with brain injuries and others with serious physical

**G** **AID STATION**

Aid stations were set up in the rear and along withdrawal routes, but there was only so much that could be done for the severely wounded given the crude facilities on offer. Many *bo doi* died during withdrawal and were buried in hidden graves. Pressure dressings and tourniquets were all that were available to keep a man from bleeding to death. Discarded American field dressings and gauze pads were washed and re-used. One indicator that an operation would soon be mounted was when large numbers of packages of sanitary napkins were bought in town stores. Local VC would buy these up to use as field dressings. If the wounded *bo doi* lived long enough to make it to an aid station, which might require at least an all-day trip, blood transfusions might be available. Blood was "donated" by rear service troops, but there was a limited supply and it remained usable only for so long. Blood was often transported in discarded US 2qt plastic bladder canteens and preserved with ice acquired by the VC from towns large enough to have an ice-making machine. At one point the Americans ceased issuing bladder canteens for this reason. Long-term use of tourniquets often resulted in gangrene, while serious gunshot wounds frequently resulted in amputation. Caffeine injections were used as a stimulant. There was little available for pain other than aspirin and marijuana; morphine was scarce. Anesthesia was simply ether, if available. What medical supplies there were mostly came from China, Warsaw Pact countries, France and American anti-war protesters, who believed they were sending the supplies to treat bomb victims in North Vietnam.

disabilities did return to the North, as food could not be sent south for them. They were not discharged or allowed to visit home, but instead were sent to camps in the highlands and in remote coastal areas. It was felt that the constant discharge of the huge numbers of disabled troops would have a detrimental affect on civilian morale. These men were allowed to write home, often for the first time since they had gone south, but they could not mention their wounds, conditions in the South, their whereabouts, or anything about the military. Their letters were heavily censored. They sometimes were able to smuggle out messages. All manner of tragic stories made the rounds. The nation was in a perpetual state of silent mourning.

The *bo doi* had been taught that the enslaved South suffered in abject poverty and the people there were exploited by imperialists and capitalists. The reality became apparent with the "liberation." It was seen what capitalism, free enterprise and freedom of choice, even in the war-torn South, had given the people in the way of improved living standards. Things were not always rosy, of course, and there were corruption and serious social problems, but compared to the North, it was a far better situation.

## COLLECTIONS, MUSEUMS AND RE-ENACTMENT

The loader prepares to drop a high-explosive round into the muzzle of an 82mm PM37 (Type 53) mortar. The NVA made wide use of this relatively portable weapon, which offered a considerable amount of firepower.

Most US Army and Marine posts have a Vietnam display in their museum with VC/NVA weapons, equipment and uniforms. The National Infantry Museum at Ft. Benning, GA and the US Military Academy Museum at West Point, NY possess excellent collections. The National Vietnam War Museum site in Mineral Wells, TX (near Dallas) was dedicated in 2004, but will not open for some years yet. Some of the best collections are in civilian collectors' hands.

The collecting of Vietnam memorabilia is a major field ranging from mementos, uniforms, equipment and insignia. Collectors are strongly urged to use caution and question the authenticity of any item represented as authentic Vietnam era. Replicas made in Vietnam, elsewhere in Asia and in the US are often sold as authentic at high prices.

There are significant numbers of Vietnam re-enactor groups in the US and other countries. Internet searches will turn up many. To oppose these groups there are a surprising number of VC/NVA re-enactor units. Replica VC/NVA uniforms and equipment are available at reasonable prices. With a heavy-duty sewing machine and the right materials it is relatively easy to make some replica NVA gear. Semi-automatic AK-47s are available while SKS and M1944 carbines can be purchased at relatively low cost. Appropriate US weapons of the era may also be used. Blank adapters and ammunition are available.

The full range of Vietnam-era weapons is also available in the form of plastic, ball bearing-firing, Airsoft replica weapons.

A group of NVA soldiers, including a machine gunner at right, photographed in 1972.

# BIBLIOGRAPHY

Bui Tin, *Following Ho Chi Minh: the Memoirs of a North Vietnamese Colonel* (Honolulu, University of Hawaii Press, 1999)

Chanoff, David and Doan van Toai, *Portrait of the Enemy* (New York, Random House, 1986)

Emering, Edward J., *Weapons and Field Gear of the North Vietnamese and Viet Cong* (Atglen, PA, Schiffer Publishing, 1998)

Lanning, Michael Lee and Cragg, Dan, *Inside the VC and the NVA: the Real Story of North Vietnam's Armed Forces* (New York, Ballantine Books, 1992)

Lulling, Darrel R., *Communist Militaria of the Vietnam War* (revised edition; Tulsa, OK, M.C.N. Press, 1980)

Katallo, Dennis C. and Bending, Allen J., *North Vietnamese Army/Viet Cong Uniforms and Field Equipment 1965–75* (Addison, IL, Miltec Enterprises, 1988)

Kellen, Konrad, *A Profile of the PAVN Soldier in South Vietnam* (Santa Monica, CA, RAND Corporation, 1965)

Marshall, S.L.A. *Bird* (New York, Warner Books, 1989)

McCoy, James W., *Secrets of the Viet Cong* (New York, Hippocrene Books, 1992)

Pike, Douglas, PAVN: *People's Army of Vietnam* (Novato, CA, Presidio Press, 1986)

Salisbury, Harrison E., *Behind the Lines: Hanoi, December 23, 1966-January 7, 1967* (London, Secker & Warburg, 1967)

Stanton, Shelby L., *Vietnam Order of Battle: a Complete Illustrated Reference to U.S. Army Combat and Support Forces in Vietnam 1961–1973* (Mechanicsburg, PA, Stackpole Books, 2003)

# INDEX

References to illustrations are shown
in **bold**